MW01256479

Cram101 Textbook Outlines to accompany:

Supervision : Concepts and Skill-Building

Samuel C. Certo, 7th Edition

A Content Technologies Inc. publication (c) 2011.

Learning System

Cram101 Textbook Outlines is a learning system. The notes in this book are the highlights of your textbook, you will never have to highlight a book again.

How to use this book. Take this book to class, it is your notebook for the lecture. The notes and highlights on the left hand side of the pages follow the outline and order of the textbook. All you have to do is follow along while your instructor presents the lecture. Circle the items emphasized in class and add other important information on the right side. With Cram101 Textbook Outlines you'll spend less time writing and more time listening. Learning becomes more efficient.

Cram101.com Online

Increase your studying efficiency by using Cram101.com's practice tests and online reference material. It is the perfect complement to Cram101 Textbook Outlines. Use self-teaching matching tests or simulate in-class testing with comprehensive multiple choice tests, or simply use Cram's true and false tests for quick review. Cram101.com even allows you to enter your in-class notes for an integrated studying format combining the textbook notes with your class notes.

Visit **www.Cram101.com**, click Sign Up at the top of the screen, and enter **DK73DW14792** in the promo code box on the registration screen. Your access to www.Cram101.com is discounted by 50% because you have purchased this book. Sign up and stop highlighting textbooks forever.

 ISBN(s): 1428878157. PUBI-1.2010128

Supervision : Concepts and Skill-Building
Samuel C. Certo, 7th

CONTENTS

1. Modern Supervision: Concepts and Skills 2
2. Ensuring High Quality and Productivity 8
3. Groups, Teams, and Powerful Meetings 24
4. Corporate Social Responsibility and Ethics 32
5. Managing Diversity 40
6. Reaching Goals: Plans and Controls 50
7. Organizing and Authority 60
8. The Supervisor as Leader 66
9. Problem Solving, Decision Making, and Creativity 76
10. Communication 84
11. Motivating Employees 90
12. Problem Employees: Counseling and Discipline 102
13. Managing Time and Stress 108
14. Managing Conflict and Change 114
15. Selecting Employees 120
16. Providing Orientation and Training 136
17. Appraising Performance 146

Chapter 1. Modern Supervision: Concepts and Skills

Labor-Management Relations Act	The Labor-Management Relations Act, 80 Pub.L. 101; 61 Stat. 136, informally the Taft-Hartley Act, is a United States federal law that monitors the activities and power of labor unions. The act, still effective, was sponsored by Senator Robert Taft and Representative Fred A. Hartley, Jr. and legislated by overriding U.S. President Harry S. Truman`s veto on June 23, 1947; labor leaders called it the `slave-labor bill` while President Truman argued it would `conflict with important principles of our democratic society,` though he would subsequently use it twelve times during his presidency.
Scientific management	Scientific management is a theory of management that analyzes and synthesizes workflows, with the objective of improving labor productivity. The core ideas of the theory were developed by Frederick Winslow Taylor in the 1880s and 1890s, and were first published in his monographs, Shop Management (1905) and The Principles of Scientific management. He began trying to discover a way for workers to increase their efficiency when he was the foreperson at the Midvale Steele Company in 1875. Taylor believed that decisions based upon tradition and rules of thumb should be replaced by precise procedures developed after careful study of an individual at work.
Henri Fayol	Henri Fayol was a French mining engineer, director of mines, and management theorist, who developed independent of the theory of Scientific Management, a general theory of business administration also known as Fayolism. He was one of the most influential contributors to modern concepts of management. Fayol was born in 1841 in a suburb of Istanbul, Turkey, where his father, an engineer, was appointed superintendent of works to build a bridge over the Golden Horn .
Needs assessment	Needs assessment is practically ubiquitous today among planners and designers, often identified as the first step in any planning or design process. Over the past four decades, there has been a proliferation of models for Needs assessment with dozens of models to choose from. What nearly all models share is a definition of Needs assessment as identification of a `gap` - but a gap in what differs from model to model.
Decision making	Decision making can be regarded as the mental processes resulting in the selection of a course of action among several alternatives. Every Decision making process produces a final choice. The output can be an action or an opinion of choice.
Brain drain	Brain drain or human capital flight is a large emigration of individuals with technical skills or knowledge, normally due to conflict, lack of opportunity, political instability, since emigrants usually take with them the fraction of value of their training sponsored by the government. It is a parallel of capital flight which refers to the same movement of financial capital.

Chapter 1. Modern Supervision: Concepts and Skills

Occupational Safety and Health Act	The Occupational Safety and Health Act is the primary federal law which governs occupational health and safety in the private sector and federal government in the United States. It was enacted by Congress in 1970 and was signed by President Richard Nixon on December 29, 1970. Its main goal is to ensure that employers provide employees with an environment free from recognized hazards, such as exposure to toxic chemicals, excessive noise levels, mechanical dangers, heat or cold stress, or unsanitary conditions. The Act can be found in the United States Code at title 29, chapter 15.
Workforce	The workforce is the labour pool in employment. It is generally used to describe those working for a single company or industry, but can also apply to a geographic region like a city, country, state, etc. The term generally excludes the employers or management, and implies those involved in manual labour.
Iron	Iron is a metallic chemical element with the symbol Fe and atomic number 26. Iron is a group 8 and period 4 element and is therefore classified as a transition metal. Iron and Iron alloys (steels) are by far the most common metals and the most common ferromagnetic materials in everyday use. Fresh Iron surfaces are lustrous and silvery-grey in color, but oxidize in air to form a red or brown coating of ferric oxide or rust.
Employment discrimination	Employment discrimination is discrimination in hiring, promotion, job assignment, termination, and compensation. It includes various types of harassment. Many jurisdictions prohibit some types of Employment discrimination, often by forbidding discrimination based on certain traits (`protected categories`).
Planning	Planning in organizations and public policy is both the organizational process of creating and maintaining a plan; and the psychological process of thinking about the activities required to create a desired goal on some scale. As such, it is a fundamental property of intelligent behavior. This thought process is essential to the creation and refinement of a plan, or integration of it with other plans, that is, it combines forecasting of developments with the preparation of scenarios of how to react to them.
Nominative determinism	Nominative determinism refers to the theory that a person`s name is given an influential role in reflecting key attributes of his job, profession, but real examples are more highly prized, the more obscure the better.

Chapter 1. Modern Supervision: Concepts and Skills

Goal	A Goal or objective is a projected state of affairs that a person or a system plans or intends to achieve--a personal or organizational desired end-point in some sort of assumed development. Many people endeavor to reach Goals within a finite time by setting deadlines. A desire or an intention becomes a Goal if and only if one activates an action for achieving it .
Virtual team	A Virtual team -- also known as a geographically dispersed team -- is a group of individuals who work across time, space, and organizational boundaries with links strengthened by webs of communication technology. They have complementary skills and are committed to a common purpose, have interdependent performance goals, and share an approach to work for which they hold themselves mutually accountable. Geographically dispersed teams allow organizations to hire and retain the best people regardless of location.
Nonverbal	Nonverbal communications (NVC) is usually understood as the process of communication through sending and receiving wordless messages. NVC can be communicated through gesture and touch (Haptic communication), by body language or posture, by facial expression and eye contact. NVC can be communicated through object communication such as clothing, hairstyles or even architecture, symbols and infographics.
Accountability	Accountability is a concept in ethics with several meanings. It is often used synonymously with such concepts as responsibility, answerability, enforcement, blameworthiness, liability, and other terms associated with the expectation of account-giving. As an aspect of governance, it has been central to discussions related to problems in both the public and private (corporation) worlds.
Delegation	Delegation is the assignment of authority and responsibility to another person to carry out specific activities. However the person who delegated the work remains accountable for the outcome of the delegated work. delegation empowers a subordinate to make decisions, i.e. it is a shift of decision-making authority from one organizational level to a lower one.
Loyalty	Loyalty is faithfulness or a devotion to a person or cause. The practice of providing discounts, prizes, or other incentives to encourage continued patronage of a business. Generally, Loyalty programs are considered less expensive to maintain than allowing customer defection or `churn`.
Virtual Workplace	A Virtual workplace is a workplace that is not located in any one physical space. Rather, several workplaces are technologically connected (via the Internet) without regard to geographic boundaries. Employees are thus able to interact and work with one another in a collaborated environment regardless of where they are in the world.

Kaizen	Kaizen refers to philosophy or practices that focus upon continuous improvement of processes in manufacturing, engineering, supporting business processes, and management. It has been applied in healthcare, government, banking, and many other industries. When used in the business sense and applied to the workplace, Kaizen refers to activities that continually improve all functions, and involves all employees from the CEO to the assembly line workers.
Productivity	Productivity is a measure of output from a production process, per unit of input. For example, lab is typically measured as a ratio of output per labor-hour, an input. productivity may be conceived of as a metric of the technical or engineering efficiency of production.
Team	A team comprises a group of people or animals linked in a common purpose. teams are especially appropriate for conducting tasks that are high in complexity and have many interdependent subtasks. A group in itself does not necessarily constitute a team.
Customer service	Customer service is the provision of service to customers before, during and after a purchase. According to Jamier L. Scott. (2002), `Customer service is a series of activities designed to enhance the level of customer satisfaction - that is, the feeling that a product or service has met the customer expectation.` Its importance varies by product, industry and customer; defective or broken merchandise can be exchanged, often only with a receipt and within a specified time frame.
Nominative determinism	Nominative determinism refers to the theory that a person`s name is given an influential role in reflecting key attributes of his job, profession, but real examples are more highly prized, the more obscure the better.
Six Sigma	Six Sigma is a business management strategy originally developed by Motorola, USA in 1981. As of 2010, it enjoys widespread application in many sectors of industry, although its application is not without controversy. Six Sigma seeks to improve the quality of process outputs by identifying and removing the causes of defects (errors) and minimizing variability in manufacturing and business processes. It uses a set of quality management methods, including statistical methods, and creates a special infrastructure of people within the organization (`Black Belts`, `Green Belts`, etc).

Process control	Process control is a statistics and engineering discipline that deals with architectures, mechanisms, and algorithms for controlling the output of a specific process.
Quality assurance	Quality assurance refers to a program for the systematic monitoring and evaluation of the various aspects of a project, service, or facility to ensure that standards of quality are being met. It is important to realize also that quality is determined by the program sponsor. Quality assurance cannot absolutely guarantee the production of quality products, unfortunately, but makes this more likely.
Quality control	Quality control is a process by which entities review the quality of all factors involved in production. This approach places an emphasis on three aspects: · Elements such as controls, job management, defined and well managed processes, performance and integrity criteria, and identification of records · Competence, such as knowledge, skills, experience, and qualifications · Soft elements, such as personnel integrity, confidence, organizational culture, motivation, team spirit, and quality relationships. The quality of the outputs is at risk if any of these three aspects is deficient in any way. Total Quality control is the most important inspection control of all in cases where, despite statistical Quality control techniques or quality improvements implemented, sales decrease.
Total quality management	Total quality management is a management concept coined by W. Edwards Deming. The basis of Total quality management is to reduce the errors produced during the manufacturing or service process, increase customer satisfaction, streamline supply chain management, aim for modernization of equipment and ensure workers have the highest level of training. One of the principal aims of Total quality management is to limit errors to 1 per 1 million units produced.
Xerox	Xerox Corporation is a global document management company which manufactures and sells a range of color and black-and-white printers, multifunction systems, photo copiers, digital production printing presses, and related consulting services and supplies. Xerox is headquartered in Norwalk, Connecticut , though its largest population of employees is based in and around Rochester, New York, the area in which the company was founded. The Xerox 914 was the first one-piece plain paper photocopier, and sold in the thousands.

Xerox was founded in 1906 in Rochester, New York as `The Haloid Company`, which originally manufactured photographic paper and equipment.

Benchmarking

Benchmarking is the process of comparing one`s business processes and performance metrics to industry bests and/or best practices from other industries. Dimensions typically measured are quality, time, and cost. Improvements from learning mean doing things better, faster, and cheaper.

ISO 9000

ISO 9000 is a family of standards for quality management systems. ISO 9000 is maintained by ISO, the International Organization for Standardization and is administered by accreditation and certification bodies. The rules are updated, as the requirements motivate changes over time. Some of the requirements in ISO 9001:2008 (which is one of the standards in the ISO 9000 family) include

· a set of procedures that cover all key processes in the business;

· monitoring processes to ensure they are effective;

· keeping adequate records;

· checking output for defects, with appropriate and corrective action where necessary;

· regularly reviewing individual processes and the quality system itself for effectiveness; and

· facilitating continual improvement

A company or organization that has been independently audited and certified to be in conformance with ISO 9001 may publicly state that it is `ISO 9001 certified` or `ISO 9001 registered`.

Economic value	The Economic value of a good or service has puzzled economists since the beginning of the discipline. First, economists tried to estimate the value of a good to an individual alone, and extend that definition to goods which can be exchanged. From this analysis came the concepts value in use and value in exchange.Wealth maximization predicts that a person will choose to obtain the good or service in the place where it is cheapest, where the amount given up is the least.Value is linked to price through the mechanism of exchange. When an economist observes an exchange, two important value functions are revealed: those of the buyer and seller. Just as the buyer reveals what he is willing to pay for a certain amount of a good, so too does the seller reveal what it costs him to give up the good.
United States	The United States of America (commonly referred to as the United States, the U.S., the United StatesA, or America) is a federal constitutional republic comprising fifty states and a federal district. The country is situated mostly in central North America, where its forty-eight contiguous states and Washington, D.C., the capital district, lie between the Pacific and Atlantic Oceans, bordered by Canada to the north and Mexico to the south. The state of Alaska is in the northwest of the continent, with Canada to its east and Russia to the west across the Bering Strait.
Brain drain	Brain drain or human capital flight is a large emigration of individuals with technical skills or knowledge, normally due to conflict, lack of opportunity, political instability, since emigrants usually take with them the fraction of value of their training sponsored by the government. It is a parallel of capital flight which refers to the same movement of financial capital.
Occupational Safety and Health Act	The Occupational Safety and Health Act is the primary federal law which governs occupational health and safety in the private sector and federal government in the United States. It was enacted by Congress in 1970 and was signed by President Richard Nixon on December 29, 1970. Its main goal is to ensure that employers provide employees with an environment free from recognized hazards, such as exposure to toxic chemicals, excessive noise levels, mechanical dangers, heat or cold stress, or unsanitary conditions. The Act can be found in the United States Code at title 29, chapter 15.
Constraint	In mathematics, a constraint is a condition that a solution to an optimization problem must satisfy. There are two types of constraints: equality constraints and inequality constraints. The set of solutions that satisfy all constraints is called the feasible set.

Trade union	A Trade union is an organization of workers who have banded together to achieve common goals such as better working conditions. The Trade union, through its leadership, bargains with the employer on behalf of union members (rank and file members) and negotiates labour contracts (collective bargaining) with employers. This may include the negotiation of wages, work rules, complaint procedures, rules governing hiring, firing and promotion of workers, benefits, workplace safety and policies.
Absenteeism	Absenteeism is a habitual pattern of absence from a duty or obligation. Frequent absence from the workplace may be indicative of poor morale or of sick building syndrome. However, many employers have implemented absence policies which make no distinction between absences for genuine illness and absence for inappropriate reasons.
Regulations	The Control of Substances Hazardous to Health regulations 2002 is a United Kingdom Statutory Instrument that stipulates general requirements on employers to protect employees and other persons from the hazards of substances used at work by risk assessment, control of exposure, health surveillance and incident planning. There are also duties on employees to take care of their own exposure to hazardous substances and prohibitions on the import of certain substances into the European Economic Area. The regulations reenacted with amendements the Control of Substances Hazardous to Work regulations 1999 and implement several European Union directives.
Overhead	In business, Overhead, Overhead cost expense refers to an ongoing expense of operating a business (also known as Operating Expenses - rent, gas/electricity, wages etc). The term Overhead is usually used to group expenses that are necessary to the continued functioning of the business, but do not directly generate profits. Overhead expenses are all costs on the income statement except for direct labor and direct materials.
Recruitment	\`Onboarding\` is a term which describes the introduction or \`induction\` process. A well-planned introduction helps new employees become fully operational quickly and is often integrated with a new company and environment. Onboarding is included in the Recruitment process for retention purposes.
Quality improvement	Quality management can be considered to have three main components: quality control, quality assurance and Quality improvement. Quality management is focused not only on product quality, but also the means to achieve it. Quality management therefore uses quality assurance and control of processes as well as products to achieve more consistent quality.
Departmentalization	Departmentalization refers to the process of grouping activities into departments.

Division of labour creates specialists who need coordination. This coordination is facilitated by grouping specialists together in departments.

Departmentalization of a personal administration

· Functional Departmentalization - Grouping activities by functions performed.

Downtime

The term Downtime is used to refer to periods when a system is unavailable. Downtime or outage duration refers to a period of time that a system fails to provide or perform its primary function. Reliability, availability, recovery, and unavailability are related concepts.

Edgar

EDGAR, the Electronic Data-Gathering, Analysis, and Retrieval system, performs automated collection, validation, indexing, acceptance, and forwarding of submissions by companies and others who are required by law to file forms with the U.S. Securities and Exchange Commission (the `SEC`). The database is freely available to the public via the Internet or FTP.
The EDGAR system typically receives in excess of 3,000 filings per day.

Not all SEC filings by public companies are available on EDGAR. Companies were phased in to EDGAR filing over a three-year period, ending 6 May 1996.

Idle

Idle is a term which generally refers to a lack of motion and/or energy.

In describing a person or machine, Idle means the act of nothing or no work. This is a person who spends his days doing nothing could be said to be `idly passing his days.` A computer processor or communication circuit is described as Idle when it is not being used by any program, application or message.

Artificial neural network

An Artificial neural network is a mathematical model or computational model that tries to simulate the structure and/or functional aspects of biological neural networks. It consists of an interconnected group of artificial neurons and processes information using a connectionist approach to computation. In most cases an Artificial neural network is an adaptive system that changes its structure based on external or internal information that flows through the network during the learning phase.

Gantt chart	A Gantt chart is a type of bar chart that illustrates a project schedule. Gantt charts illustrate the start and finish dates of the terminal elements and summary elements of a project. Terminal elements and summary elements comprise the work breakdown structure of the project. Some Gantt charts also show the dependency (i.e. precedence network) relationships between activities.
Workforce	The workforce is the labour pool in employment. It is generally used to describe those working for a single company or industry, but can also apply to a geographic region like a city, country, state, etc. The term generally excludes the employers or management, and implies those involved in manual labour.
Motivation	Motivation is the activation or energization of goal-oriented behavior. Motivation may be internal or external. The term is generally used for humans but, theoretically, it can also be used to describe the causes for animal behavior as well.
Payback period	Payback period in capital budgeting refers to the period of time required for the return on an investment to `repay` the sum of the original investment. For example, a $1000 investment which returned $500 per year would have a two year Payback period. The time value of money is not taken into account.
Rate of return	In finance, Rate of return also known as return on investment (ROI), rate of profit or sometimes just return, is the ratio of money gained or lost (whether realized or unrealized) on an investment relative to the amount of money invested. The amount of money gained or lost may be referred to as interest, profit/loss, gain/loss, or net income/loss. The money invested may be referred to as the asset, capital, principal, or the cost basis of the investment.
Reduce	For example, it is fairly easy for a top executive to reduce the price of his/her company`s stock - due to information asymmetry. The executive can accelerate accounting of expected expenses, delay accounting of expected revenue, engage in off balance sheet transactions to make the company`s profitability appear temporarily poorer, or simply promote and report severely conservative (eg. pessimistic) estimates of future earnings.
Turnover	In a human resources context, Turnover is the rate at which an employer gains and loses employees. Simple ways to describe it are `how long employees tend to stay` or `the rate of traffic through the revolving door.` Turnover is measured for individual companies and for their industry as a whole. If an employer is said to have a high Turnover relative to its competitors, it means that employees of that company have a shorter average tenure than those of other companies in the same industry.

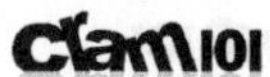

Offshoring	Offshoring describes the relocation by a company of a business process from one country to another--typically an operational process, such as manufacturing, or supporting processes, such as accounting. Even state governments employ Offshoring.
Outsourcing	Outsourcing often refers to the process of contracting to a third-party. While Outsourcing may be viewed as a component to the growing division of labor encompassing all societies, the term did not enter the English-speaking lexicon until the 1980s. Since the 1980s, transnational corporations have increased subcontracting across national boundaries.

Chapter 3. Groups, Teams, and Powerful Meetings

Group	In business, a group, business group, corporate group) alliance is most commonly a legal entity that is a type of conglomerate or holding company consisting of a parent company and subsidiaries. Typical examples are Adidas group or Icelandair group. In United Arab Emirates, Business group can also be knows as Trade association.
Team	A team comprises a group of people or animals linked in a common purpose. teams are especially appropriate for conducting tasks that are high in complexity and have many interdependent subtasks. A group in itself does not necessarily constitute a team.
Brain drain	Brain drain or human capital flight is a large emigration of individuals with technical skills or knowledge, normally due to conflict, lack of opportunity, political instability, since emigrants usually take with them the fraction of value of their training sponsored by the government. It is a parallel of capital flight which refers to the same movement of financial capital.
Occupational Safety and Health Act	The Occupational Safety and Health Act is the primary federal law which governs occupational health and safety in the private sector and federal government in the United States. It was enacted by Congress in 1970 and was signed by President Richard Nixon on December 29, 1970. Its main goal is to ensure that employers provide employees with an environment free from recognized hazards, such as exposure to toxic chemicals, excessive noise levels, mechanical dangers, heat or cold stress, or unsanitary conditions. The Act can be found in the United States Code at title 29, chapter 15.
Cohesiveness	Group Cohesiveness is the force bringing group members closer together. Cohesiveness has two dimensions: emotional (or personal) and task-related. The emotional aspect of Cohesiveness, which was studied more often, is derived from the connection that members feel to other group members and to their group as a whole.
Conflict	Many NGOs and independent groups attempt to monitor the situation of ongoing Conflicts. Unfortunately, the definitions of war, Conflict, armed struggle, revolution and all these words which describe violent opposition between States or armed organised groups, are not precise enough to distinguish one from another. For example, the word terrorism is used indifferently by many governments to delegitimate every kind of armed revolt and, at the same time, by many rebel groups to delegitimate the armed repression of sovereign.
Role conflict	Role conflict is a conflict among the roles corresponding to two or more statuses.

Role conflict is a special form of social conflict that takes place when one is forced to take on two different and incompatible roles at the same time.

Absenteeism

Absenteeism is a habitual pattern of absence from a duty or obligation.
Frequent absence from the workplace may be indicative of poor morale or of sick building syndrome. However, many employers have implemented absence policies which make no distinction between absences for genuine illness and absence for inappropriate reasons.

Leadership

In response to the criticism of the trait approach, theorists began to research Leadership as a set of behaviors, evaluating the behavior of `successful` leaders, determining a behavior taxonomy and identifying broad Leadership styles. David McClelland, for example, saw Leadership skills, not so much as a set of traits, but as a pattern of motives. He claimed that successful leaders will tend to have a high need for power, a low need for affiliation, and a high level of what he called activity inhibition (one might call it self-control).

Motivation

Motivation is the activation or energization of goal-oriented behavior. Motivation may be internal or external. The term is generally used for humans but, theoretically, it can also be used to describe the causes for animal behavior as well.

Market

A Market is any one of a variety of different systems, institutions, procedures, social relations and infrastructures whereby persons trade, and goods and services are exchanged, forming part of the economy. It is an arrangement that allows buyers and sellers to exchange things. Markets vary in size, range, geographic scale, location, types and variety of human communities, as well as the types of goods and services traded.

Team leader

A Team leader is someone (or in certain cases there may be multiple Team leaders) who provides guidance, instruction, direction, leadership to a group of other individuals (the team) for the purpose of achieving a key result or group of aligned results. The Team leader reports to a project manager. The Team leader monitors the quantitative and qualitative result that is to be achieved.

Enabling

Enabling is a term with a double meaning.
As a positive term, it references patterns of interaction which allow individuals to develop and grow. These may be on any scale, for example within the family, or in wider society as `Enabling acts` designed to empower some group, or create a new authority for a (usually governmental) body.

Productivity

Productivity is a measure of output from a production process, per unit of input. For example, lab is typically measured as a ratio of output per labor-hour, an input. productivity may be conceived of as a metric of the technical or engineering efficiency of production.

Team building	Work environments tend to focus on individuals and personal goals, with reward ' recognition singling out the achievements of individual employees. `How to create effective teams is a challenge in every organization` Team building can also refer to the process of selecting or creating a team from scratch. Reasons for Team building include · Improving communication · Making the workplace more enjoyable · Motivating a team · Getting to know each other · Getting everyone `onto the same page`, including goal setting · Teaching the team self-regulation strategies · Helping participants to learn more about themselves (strengths and weaknesses) · Identifying and utilizing the strengths of team members · Improving team productivity · Practicing effective collaboration with team members What are Team building Exercises and what is their purpose? Team building exercises consist of a variety of tasks designed to develop group members and their ability to work together effectively. There are many types of Team building activities that range from kids games to games that involve novel complex tasks and are designed for specific needs.

Self-assessment	Self-assessment in an organisational setting, according to the EFQM definition, refers to a comprehensive, systematic and regular review of an organization`s activities and results referenced against the EFQM Excellence Model. The Self-assessment process allows the organization to discern clearly its strengths and areas in which improvements can be made and culminates in planned improvement actions which are then monitored for progress. Self-assessment in an educational setting involves students making judgments about their own work.

Corporate social responsibility	Corporate social responsibility is a form of corporate self-regulation integrated into a business model. Ideally, Corporate social responsibility policy would function as a built-in, self-regulating mechanism whereby business would monitor and ensure its support to law, ethical standards, and international norms. Consequently, business would embrace responsibility for the impact of its activities on the environment, consumers, employees, communities, stakeholders and all other members of the public sphere.
Absenteeism	Absenteeism is a habitual pattern of absence from a duty or obligation. Frequent absence from the workplace may be indicative of poor morale or of sick building syndrome. However, many employers have implemented absence policies which make no distinction between absences for genuine illness and absence for inappropriate reasons.
Type I error	In statistics, the terms Type I error and type II error (β error) are used to describe possible errors made in a statistical decision process. In 1928, Jerzy Neyman (1894-1981) and Egon Pearson (1895-1980), both eminent statisticians, discussed the problems associated with `deciding whether or not a particular sample may be judged as likely to have been randomly drawn from a certain population` (1928/1967, p.1): and identified `two sources of error`, namely: Type I (α): reject the null hypothesis when the null hypothesis is true, and Type II (β): fail to reject the null hypothesis when the null hypothesis is false In 1930, they elaborated on these two sources of error, remarking that `in testing hypotheses two considerations must be kept in view, (1) we must be able to reduce the chance of rejecting a true hypothesis to as low a value as desired; (2) the test must be so devised that it will reject the hypothesis tested when it is likely to be false.` Scientists recognize two different sorts of error: · Statistical error: the difference between a computed, estimated, or measured value and the true, specified, or theoretically correct value that is caused by random, and inherently unpredictable fluctuations in the measurement apparatus or the system being studied. · Systematic error: the difference between a computed, estimated, or measured value and the true, specified, or theoretically correct value that is caused by non-random fluctuations from an unknown source , and which, once identified, can usually be eliminated.

Statisticians speak of two significant sorts of statistical error. The context is that there is a `null hypothesis` which corresponds to a presumed default `state of nature`, e.g., that an individual is free of disease, that an accused is innocent, or that a potential login candidate is not authorized.

Corruption

The word corrupt when used as an adverb literally means `utterly broken`. In modern English usage the words Corruption and corrupt have many meanings:

· Political Corruption: the abuse of public power, office, or resources by government officials or employees for personal gain, e.g. by extortion, soliciting or offering bribes.

· Corporate Corruption: corporate criminality and the abuse of power by corporation officials, either internally or externally.

· Putrefaction: the natural process of decomposition in the human and animal body following death.

· Data Corruption: an unintended change to data in storage or in transit.

· Linguistic Corruption: the change in meaning to a language or a text introduced by cumulative errors in transcription as changes in the language speakers` comprehension.

· Bribery in politics, business, or sport .
Institutions dealing with political Corruption

· Transparency International

· Group of States Against Corruption , a body established under the Council of Europe to monitor the implementation of instruments adopted by member states to combat political Corruption.
Entertainment with Corruption themes

· Metroid Prime 3: Corruption, a Wii game.

· Corrupt (film), a 1981 film starring Harvey Keitel and John Lydon.

· Corrupt (1999 film), a 1999 film starring Ice-T and Silkk The Shocker.

· Corrupt (Angel), an unproduced teleplay written for the television program Angel.

· Kurupt, a rapper

· Corruption, a 1988 computer game by Magnetic Scrolls.

· Corrupted, a Japanese doom-metal band. .

Business value

In management, Business value is an informal term that includes all forms of value that determine the health and well-being of the firm in the long-run. Business value expands concept of value of the firm beyond economic value (also known as economic profit, Economic value added, and Shareholder value) to include other forms of value such as employee value, customer value, supplier value, channel partner value, alliance partner value, managerial value, and societal value. Many of these forms of value are not directly measured in monetary terms.

Loyalty

Loyalty is faithfulness or a devotion to a person or cause.
The practice of providing discounts, prizes, or other incentives to encourage continued patronage of a business. Generally, Loyalty programs are considered less expensive to maintain than allowing customer defection or `churn`.

Decision making

Decision making can be regarded as the mental processes resulting in the selection of a course of action among several alternatives. Every Decision making process produces a final choice. The output can be an action or an opinion of choice.

Communications management

Communications management is the systematic planning, implementing, monitoring, and revision of all the channels of communication within an organization, and between organizations; it also includes the organization and dissemination of new communication directives connected with an organization, network, designing internal and external communications directives, and managing the flow of information, including online communication. New technology forces constant innovation on the part of communications managers.

Sarbanes-Oxley Act	The Sarbanes-Oxley Act of 2002 (Pub.L. 107-204, 116 Stat. 745, enacted July 30, 2002), also known as the `Public Company Accounting Reform and Investor Protection Act` (in the Senate) and `Corporate and Auditing Accountability and Responsibility Act` (in the House) and commonly called Sarbanes-Oxley, Sarbox or SOX, is a United States federal law enacted on July 30, 2002, as a reaction to a number of major corporate and accounting scandals including those affecting Enron, Tyco International, Adelphia, Peregrine Systems and WorldCom. These scandals, which cost investors billions of dollars when the share prices of affected companies collapsed, shook public confidence in the nation`s securities markets. Named after sponsors U.S. Senator Paul Sarbanes (D-MD) and U.S. Representative Michael G. Oxley (R-OH), the act was approved by the House by a vote of 423-3 and by the Senate 99-0. President George W. Bush signed it into law, stating it included `the most far-reaching reforms of American business practices since the time of Franklin D. Roosevelt.` The legislation set new or enhanced standards for all U.S. public company boards, management and public accounting firms.

Revenue	In business, Revenue is income that a company receives from its normal business activities, usually from the sale of goods and services to customers. In many countries, such as the United Kingdom, Revenue is referred to as turnover. Some companies receive Revenue from interest, dividends or royalties paid to them by other companies.
United States	The United States of America (commonly referred to as the United States, the U.S., the United StatesA, or America) is a federal constitutional republic comprising fifty states and a federal district. The country is situated mostly in central North America, where its forty-eight contiguous states and Washington, D.C., the capital district, lie between the Pacific and Atlantic Oceans, bordered by Canada to the north and Mexico to the south. The state of Alaska is in the northwest of the continent, with Canada to its east and Russia to the west across the Bering Strait.
Workforce	The workforce is the labour pool in employment. It is generally used to describe those working for a single company or industry, but can also apply to a geographic region like a city, country, state, etc. The term generally excludes the employers or management, and implies those involved in manual labour.
Artificial neural network	An Artificial neural network is a mathematical model or computational model that tries to simulate the structure and/or functional aspects of biological neural networks. It consists of an interconnected group of artificial neurons and processes information using a connectionist approach to computation. In most cases an Artificial neural network is an adaptive system that changes its structure based on external or internal information that flows through the network during the learning phase.
Glass ceiling	In economics, the term Glass ceiling refers to situations where the advancement of a qualified person within the hierarchy of an organization is stopped at a lower level because of some form of discrimination, most commonly sexism or racism, but since the term was coined, \`Glass ceiling\` has also come to describe the limited advancement of the deaf, blind, disabled, and aged. It is believed to be an unofficial, invisible barrier that prevents women and minorities from advancing in businesses. This situation is referred to as a \`ceiling\` as there is a limitation blocking upward advancement, and \`glass\` (transparent) because the limitation is not immediately apparent and is normally an unwritten and unofficial policy.
Nielsen	Nielsen Danish pronunciation: [Ë̂nelsn], is a Danish patronymic surname, literally meaning son of Niels, Niels being the Danish version of the Greek male given name ΝικΪŒλαος, Nikolaos . It is the second most common surname in Denmark, shared by about 5% of the population. It is also used in Norway, although the form Nilsen is more common.

Sexual harassment	Sexual harassment is intimidation, bullying or coercion of a sexual nature, Sexual harassment may be illegal. It includes a range of behavior from seemingly mild transgressions and annoyances to actual sexual abuse or sexual assault.
Xerox	Xerox Corporation is a global document management company which manufactures and sells a range of color and black-and-white printers, multifunction systems, photo copiers, digital production printing presses, and related consulting services and supplies. Xerox is headquartered in Norwalk, Connecticut , though its largest population of employees is based in and around Rochester, New York, the area in which the company was founded. The Xerox 914 was the first one-piece plain paper photocopier, and sold in the thousands. Xerox was founded in 1906 in Rochester, New York as `The Haloid Company`, which originally manufactured photographic paper and equipment.
Ownership	Ownership is the state or fact of exclusive rights and control over property, which may be an object, land/real estate or intellectual property. An Ownership right is also referred to as title. The concept of Ownership has existed for thousands of years and in all cultures.
Employment	Employment is a contract between two parties, one being the employer and the other being the employee. An employee may be defined as: `A person in the service of another under any contract of hire, express or implied, oral or written, where the employer has the power or right to control and direct the employee in the material details of how the work is to be performed.` Black`s Law Dictionary page 471 (5th ed. 1979). In a commercial setting, the employer conceives of a productive activity, generally with the intention of generating a profit, and the employee contributes labour to the enterprise, usually in return for payment of wages.
Equal	EQUAL was the `Community Initiative` within the European Social Fund of the European Union. It concerned `transnational co-operation to promote new means of combating all forms of discrimination and inEQUALities in connection with the labour market`. It ran from 2001 till 2007 with a budget of some â‚¬3 billion of EU resources, matched by a similar sum from national resources.
Equal Employment Opportunity	The term Equal Employment Opportunity was created by President Lyndon B. Johnson when he signed Executive Order 11246 on September 24, 1965, created to prohibit federal contractors from discriminating against employees on the basis of race, sex, creed, religion, color, or national origin. In more recent times, most employers have also added sexual orientation to the list of non-discrimination. The Executive Order also required contractors to implement affirmative action plans to increase the participation of minorities and women in the workplace.

Equal Employment Opportunity Commission	The U.S. Equal Employment Opportunity Commission is an independent federal agency that enforces laws against workplace discrimination. The Equal Employment Opportunity Commission investigates discrimination complaints based on an individual`s race, color, national origin, religion, sex, sexual orentation, age, disability and retaliation for reporting and/or opposing a discriminatory practice. It is empowered to file discrimination suits against employers on behalf of alleged victims and to adjudicate claims of discrimination brought against federal agencies.
Employment discrimination	Employment discrimination is discrimination in hiring, promotion, job assignment, termination, and compensation. It includes various types of harassment. Many jurisdictions prohibit some types of Employment discrimination, often by forbidding discrimination based on certain traits (`protected categories`).
Age Discrimination in Employment Act	The Age Discrimination in Employment Act of 1967, Pub. L. No. 90-202, 81 Stat. 602 (Dec. 15, 1967), codified as Chapter 14 of Title 29 of the United States Code, 29 U.S.C. Â§ 621 through 29 U.S.C. Â§ 634 (ADEA), prohibits employment discrimination against persons 40 years of age or older in the United States). The law also sets standards for pensions and benefits provided by employers and requires that information about the needs of older workers be provided to the general public.
Age Discrimination in Employment Act of 1967	The Age Discrimination in Employment Act of 1967, Pub. L. No. 90-202, 81 Stat. 602 (Dec. 15, 1967), codified as Chapter 14 of Title 29 of the United States Code, 29 U.S.C. Â§ 621 through 29 U.S.C. Â§ 634 (ADEA), prohibits employment discrimination against persons 40 years of age or older in the United States). The law also sets standards for pensions and benefits provided by employers and requires that information about the needs of older workers be provided to the general public.
Group	In business, a group, business group, corporate group) alliance is most commonly a legal entity that is a type of conglomerate or holding company consisting of a parent company and subsidiaries. Typical examples are Adidas group or Icelandair group. In United Arab Emirates, Business group can also be knows as Trade association.
Nonverbal	Nonverbal communications (NVC) is usually understood as the process of communication through sending and receiving wordless messages. NVC can be communicated through gesture and touch (Haptic communication), by body language or posture, by facial expression and eye contact. NVC can be communicated through object communication such as clothing, hairstyles or even architecture, symbols and infographics.

Nonverbal communication	Nonverbal communication is usually understood as the process of communication through sending and receiving wordless messages. i.e., language is not the only source of communication, there are other means also. NVC can be communicated through gestures and touch (Haptic communication), by body language or posture, by facial expression and eye contact.
Diversity training	Diversity training is training for the purpose of increasing participants` cultural awareness, knowledge, and skills, which is based on the assumption that the training will benefit an organization by protecting against civil rights violations, increasing the inclusion of different identity groups, and promoting better teamwork. Diversity training has been a controversial issue, due to moral considerations as well as questioned efficiency or even counterproductivity. According to Michael Bird, many project managers may feel that they are treading new territory as they lead project teams made of individuals from different cultures, heterogeneous mixes, and differing demographics.
Jargon	Jargon is terminology which is especially defined in relationship to a specific activity, profession, or group. The philosophe Condillac observed in 1782 that `Every science requires a special language because every science has its own ideas.` As a rationalist member of the Enlightenment he continued, `It seems that one ought to begin by composing this language, but people begin by speaking and writing and the language remains to be composed.` In other words, the term covers the language used by people who work in a particular area or who have a common interest. Much like slang, it can develop as a kind of short-hand, to express ideas that are frequently discussed between members of a group, though it can also be developed deliberately using chosen terms.
Civil Rights Act of 1991	The Civil Rights Act of 1991 is a United States statute that was passed in response to a series of United States Supreme Court decisions which limited the rights of employees who had sued their employers for discrimination. The Act represented the first effort since the passage of the Civil Rights Act of 1964 to modify some of the basic procedural and substantive rights provided by federal law in employment discrimination cases. It provided for the right to trial by jury on discrimination claims and introduced the possibility of emotional distress damages, while limiting the amount that a jury could award.

Equal Pay Act of 1963	The Equal Pay Act of 1963, Pub. L. No. 88-38, 77 Stat. 56, (June 10, 1963) codified at 29 U.S.C. Â§ 206(d), is a United States federal law amending the Fair Labor Standards Act, aimed at abolishing wage differentials based on sex. In passing the bill, Congress denounces sex discrimination for the following reasons: · It depresses wages and living standards for employees necessary for their health and efficiency; · it prevents the maximum utilization of the available labor resources · it tends to cause labor disputes, thereby burdening, affecting, and obstructing commerce; · it burdens commerce and the free flow of goods in commerce; and · it constitutes an unfair method of competition. The law provides (in part) that: No employer having employees subject to any provisions of this section [section 206 of title 29 of the United States Code] shall discriminate, within any establishment in which such employees are employed, between employees on the basis of sex by paying wages to employees in such establishment at a rate less than the rate at which he pays wages to employees of the opposite sex in such establishment for equal work on jobs[,] the performance of which requires equal skill, effort, and responsibility, and which are performed under similar working conditions, except where such payment is made pursuant to (i) a seniority system; (ii) a merit system; (iii) a system which measures earnings by quantity or quality of production; or (iv) a differential based on any other factor other than sex [.
Rehabilitation Act	The U.S. Rehabilitation Act of 1973 prohibits discrimination on the basis of disability in programs conducted by Federal agencies, in programs receiving Federal financial assistance, in Federal employment, and in the employment practices of Federal contractors. The standards for determining employment discrimination under the Rehabilitation Act are the same as those used in title I of the Americans with Disabilities Act.
Team	A team comprises a group of people or animals linked in a common purpose. teams are especially appropriate for conducting tasks that are high in complexity and have many interdependent subtasks. A group in itself does not necessarily constitute a team.

Chapter 6. Reaching Goals: Plans and Controls

Goal	A Goal or objective is a projected state of affairs that a person or a system plans or intends to achieve--a personal or organizational desired end-point in some sort of assumed development. Many people endeavor to reach Goals within a finite time by setting deadlines. A desire or an intention becomes a Goal if and only if one activates an action for achieving it .
Planning	Planning in organizations and public policy is both the organizational process of creating and maintaining a plan; and the psychological process of thinking about the activities required to create a desired goal on some scale. As such, it is a fundamental property of intelligent behavior. This thought process is essential to the creation and refinement of a plan, or integration of it with other plans, that is, it combines forecasting of developments with the preparation of scenarios of how to react to them.
File sharing	File sharing is the practice of distributing or providing access to digitally stored information, such as computer programs, multi-media (audio, video), documents, transmission, and distribution models. Common methods are manual sharing using removable media, centralized computer file server installations on computer networks, World Wide Web-based hyperlinked documents, and the use of distributed peer-to-peer (P2P) networking.
Nominative determinism	Nominative determinism refers to the theory that a person`s name is given an influential role in reflecting key attributes of his job, profession, but real examples are more highly prized, the more obscure the better.
Operational definition	An Operational definition is a demonstration of a process - such as a variable, term, or object - in terms of the specific process or set of validation tests used to determine its presence and quantity. The term was coined by Percy Williams Bridgman . Properties described in this manner must be sufficiently accessible, so that persons other than the definer may independently measure or test for them at will.
Operational planning	An Operational planning is a subset of strategic work plan. It describes short-term ways of achieving milestones and explains how, or what portion of, a strategic plan will be put into operation during a given operational period, in the case of commercial application, a fiscal year or another given budgetary term. An operational plan is the basis for, and justification of an annual operating budget request.

Strategic planning	Strategic planning is an organization`s process of defining its strategy, or direction, and making decisions on allocating its resources to pursue this strategy, including its capital and people. Various business analysis techniques can be used in Strategic planning, including SWOT analysis (Strengths, Weaknesses, Opportunities, and Threats), PEST analysis (Political, Economic, Social, and Technological), STEER analysis (Socio-cultural, Technological, Economic, Ecological, and Regulatory factors), and EPISTEL . Strategic planning is the formal consideration of an organization`s future course. All Strategic planning deals with at least one of three key questions:  · `What do we do?`  · `For whom do we do it?`  · `How do we excel?` In business Strategic planning, the third question is better phrased `How can we beat or avoid competition?`.
Hostile work environment	A Hostile work environment exists when an employee experiences workplace harassment and fears going to work because of the offensive, intimidating, religion, sex, national origin, age, disability, veteran status, or, in some jurisdictions, sexual orientation, political affiliation, citizenship status, marital status, or personal appearance. Hostile work environment is also one of the two legal categories of sexual harassment. A Hostile work environment may also be defined as when a boss or manager begins to engage in a manner designed to make you quit in retaliation for your actions.
Procedure	A procedure is a specified series of actions or operations which have to be executed in the same manner in order to always obtain the same result under the same circumstances (for example, emergency procedures). Less precisely speaking, this word can indicate a sequence of activities, tasks, steps, decisions, calculations and processes, that when undertaken in the sequence laid down produces the described result, product or outcome. A procedure usually induces a change.
Management by objectives	Management by objectives is a process of agreeing upon objectives within an organization so that management and employees agree to the objectives and understand what they are in the organization.

	The term `Management by objectives` was first popularized by Peter Drucker in his 1954 book `The Practice of Management`. The essence of Management by objectives is participative goal setting, choosing course of actions and decision making. An important part of the Management by objectives is the measurement and the comparison of the employee`s actual performance with the standards set. Ideally, when employees themselves have been involved with the goal setting and choosing the course of action to be followed by them, they are more likely to fulfill their responsibilities.
Brain drain	Brain drain or human capital flight is a large emigration of individuals with technical skills or knowledge, normally due to conflict, lack of opportunity, political instability, since emigrants usually take with them the fraction of value of their training sponsored by the government. It is a parallel of capital flight which refers to the same movement of financial capital.
Occupational Safety and Health Act	The Occupational Safety and Health Act is the primary federal law which governs occupational health and safety in the private sector and federal government in the United States. It was enacted by Congress in 1970 and was signed by President Richard Nixon on December 29, 1970. Its main goal is to ensure that employers provide employees with an environment free from recognized hazards, such as exposure to toxic chemicals, excessive noise levels, mechanical dangers, heat or cold stress, or unsanitary conditions. The Act can be found in the United States Code at title 29, chapter 15.
Resources	A resource is any physical or virtual entity of limited availability, or anything used to help one earn a living. In most cases, commercial or even ethic factors require resource allocation through resource management. As resources are very useful, we attach some information value to them.
Broadcast programming	Broadcast programming is the practice of organizing television or radio programs in a daily, weekly, or season-long schedule. Modern broadcasters regularly change the scheduling of their programs to build an audience for a new show, retain that audience, or compete with other broadcasters` programs.

	Television scheduling strategies are employed to give programs the best possible chance of attracting and retaining an audience.
Gantt chart	A Gantt chart is a type of bar chart that illustrates a project schedule. Gantt charts illustrate the start and finish dates of the terminal elements and summary elements of a project. Terminal elements and summary elements comprise the work breakdown structure of the project. Some Gantt charts also show the dependency (i.e. precedence network) relationships between activities.
Program evaluation	Program evaluation is a systematic method for collecting, analyzing, and using information to answer basic questions about projects, policies and programs. Program evaluation is used in the public and private sector and is taught in numerous universities. Evaluation became particularly relevant in the U.S. in the 1960s during the period of the Great Society social programs associated with the Kennedy and Johnson administrations.
Team	A team comprises a group of people or animals linked in a common purpose. teams are especially appropriate for conducting tasks that are high in complexity and have many interdependent subtasks. A group in itself does not necessarily constitute a team.
Absenteeism	Absenteeism is a habitual pattern of absence from a duty or obligation. Frequent absence from the workplace may be indicative of poor morale or of sick building syndrome. However, many employers have implemented absence policies which make no distinction between absences for genuine illness and absence for inappropriate reasons.
Evaluation	Evaluation is systematic determination of merit, worth, and significance of something or someone using criteria against a set of standards. Evaluation often is used to characterize and appraise subjects of interest in a wide range of human enterprises, including the arts, criminal justice, foundations and non-profit organizations, government, health care, and other human services.
Variance	In probability theory and statistics, the Variance of a random variable, probability distribution, or sample is a measure of statistical dispersion, averaging the squared deviations of its possible values from the expected value (mean.) Whereas the mean is a way to describe the location of a distribution, the Variance is a way to capture its scale or degree of being spread out. The unit of Variance is the square of the unit of the original variable.

Artificial neural network	An Artificial neural network is a mathematical model or computational model that tries to simulate the structure and/or functional aspects of biological neural networks. It consists of an interconnected group of artificial neurons and processes information using a connectionist approach to computation. In most cases an Artificial neural network is an adaptive system that changes its structure based on external or internal information that flows through the network during the learning phase.
Overtime	Overtime is the amount of time someone works beyond normal working hours. Normal hours may be determined in several ways: · by custom (what is considered healthy or reasonable by society), · by practices of a given trade or profession, · by legislation, · by agreement between employers and workers or their representatives. Most nations have Overtime laws designed to dissuade or prevent employers from forcing their employees to work excessively long hours. These laws may take into account other considerations than the humanitarian, such as increasing the overall level of employment in the economy.
Symptom	A symptom is a departure from normal function or feeling which is noticed by a patient, indicating the presence of disease or abnormality. A symptom is subjective, observed by the patient, and not measured. symptoms may be chronic, relapsing or remitting.
Feedback	Feedback describes the situation when output from (or information about the result of) an event or phenomenon in the past will influence an occurrence or occurrences of the same (i.e. same defined) event / phenomenon in the present or future. When an event is part of a chain of cause-and-effect that forms a circuit or loop, then the event is said to `feed back` into itself.
Performance report	A performance report is a report on the performance of something. They are routinely produced by government bodies which, being financed by public money, are required to show that the money was spent efficiently and usefully. Such reports will contain performance indicators which measure the achievements of the organisation and its programmes.

Departmentalization	Departmentalization refers to the process of grouping activities into departments. Division of labour creates specialists who need coordination. This coordination is facilitated by grouping specialists together in departments. Departmentalization of a personal administration · Functional Departmentalization - Grouping activities by functions performed.
Organizational structure	An Organizational structure is a mainly hierarchical concept of subordination of entities that collaborate and contribute to serve one common aim. Organizations are a variant of clustered entities. An organization can be structured in many different ways and styles, depending on their objectives and ambience.
Intrapreneurship	In 1992, The American Heritage Dictionary brought intrapreneurism into the main stream by adding intrapreneur to its dictionary, defining it as `a person within a large corporation who takes direct responsibility for turning an idea into a profitable finished product through assertive risk-taking and innovation`. Intrapreneurship was a concept here to stay. The term itself dates to the 1983 PhD dissertation by Burgelman and later defined in a 1985 book by Gifford Pinchot III, `Intrapreneuring`; a revised edition, entitled `Intrapreneuring in Action` is currently published.
Line authority	Line authority is the power to give orders to subordinates. It contrasts with Staff Authority, which is the authority to advise but not command others. Line managers are responsible for attaining the organization`s goals as efficiently as possible.
Accountability	Accountability is a concept in ethics with several meanings. It is often used synonymously with such concepts as responsibility, answerability, enforcement, blameworthiness, liability, and other terms associated with the expectation of account-giving. As an aspect of governance, it has been central to discussions related to problems in both the public and private (corporation) worlds.

Resources	A resource is any physical or virtual entity of limited availability, or anything used to help one earn a living. In most cases, commercial or even ethic factors require resource allocation through resource management. As resources are very useful, we attach some information value to them.
Group	In business, a group, business group, corporate group) alliance is most commonly a legal entity that is a type of conglomerate or holding company consisting of a parent company and subsidiaries. Typical examples are Adidas group or Icelandair group. In United Arab Emirates, Business group can also be knows as Trade association.
Absenteeism	Absenteeism is a habitual pattern of absence from a duty or obligation. Frequent absence from the workplace may be indicative of poor morale or of sick building syndrome. However, many employers have implemented absence policies which make no distinction between absences for genuine illness and absence for inappropriate reasons.
Planning	Planning in organizations and public policy is both the organizational process of creating and maintaining a plan; and the psychological process of thinking about the activities required to create a desired goal on some scale. As such, it is a fundamental property of intelligent behavior. This thought process is essential to the creation and refinement of a plan, or integration of it with other plans, that is, it combines forecasting of developments with the preparation of scenarios of how to react to them.
Span of control	Span of control is a term originating in military organization theory, but now used more commonly in business management, particularly human resource management. Span of control refers to the number of subordinates a supervisor has. In the hierarchical business organization of the past it was not uncommon to see average spans of 1 to 4 or even less. That is, one manager supervised four employees on average. In the 1980s corporate leaders flattened many organizational structures causing average spans to move closer to 1 to 10. That was made possible primarily by the development of inexpensive information technology. As information technogy was developed capable of easing many middle manager tasks - tasks like collecting, manipulating and presenting operational information - upper managers found they could hire fewer middle managers to do more work managing more subordinates for less money.

Delegation	Delegation is the assignment of authority and responsibility to another person to carry out specific activities. However the person who delegated the work remains accountable for the outcome of the delegated work. delegation empowers a subordinate to make decisions, i.e. it is a shift of decision-making authority from one organizational level to a lower one.
Empowerment	Empowerment refers to increasing the spiritual, political, social, or economic strength of individuals and communities. It often involves the empowered developing confidence in their own capacities.
	The term Empowerment covers a vast landscape of meanings, interpretations, definitions and disciplines ranging from psychology and philosophy to the highly commercialized self-help industry and motivational sciences.

Sexual harassment	Sexual harassment is intimidation, bullying or coercion of a sexual nature, Sexual harassment may be illegal. It includes a range of behavior from seemingly mild transgressions and annoyances to actual sexual abuse or sexual assault.
Customer service	Customer service is the provision of service to customers before, during and after a purchase. According to Jamier L. Scott. (2002), `Customer service is a series of activities designed to enhance the level of customer satisfaction - that is, the feeling that a product or service has met the customer expectation.` Its importance varies by product, industry and customer; defective or broken merchandise can be exchanged, often only with a receipt and within a specified time frame.
Locus of control	Locus of control in social psychology refers to the extent to which individuals believe that they can control events that affect them. Understanding of the concept was developed by Julian B. Rotter in 1954, and has since become an important aspect of personality studies. Individuals with a high internal Locus of control believe that events result primarily from their own behavior and actions.
Planning	Planning in organizations and public policy is both the organizational process of creating and maintaining a plan; and the psychological process of thinking about the activities required to create a desired goal on some scale. As such, it is a fundamental property of intelligent behavior. This thought process is essential to the creation and refinement of a plan, or integration of it with other plans, that is, it combines forecasting of developments with the preparation of scenarios of how to react to them.
Self-confidence	The socio-psychological concept of Self-confidence relates to self-assuredness in one`s personal judgment, ability, power, etc., sometimes manifested excessively. Another definition is the belief of believing in you; to believe that one is able to accomplish what one sets out to do, to overcome obstacles and challenges (Peixe, 2009). Compare:

· confidence (often equivalent to Self-confidence)

· hubris (excessive Self-confidence)

· self-esteem (conceit, or favourable opinion of oneself, or self-acceptance).

Lack of Self-confidence is called timidness or timidity.

Laissez-faire

In economics, Laissez-faire means allowing industry to be free of government restriction, especially restrictions in the form of tarriffs and government monopolies. The phrase is French, literally meaning `let the people do as they please` Sometimes, but rarely, the phrase is used to describe a form of philosophic anarchism.

The exact origins of the term Laissez-faire as a slogan of economic liberalism are uncertain.

Leadership

In response to the criticism of the trait approach, theorists began to research Leadership as a set of behaviors, evaluating the behavior of `successful` leaders, determining a behavior taxonomy and identifying broad Leadership styles. David McClelland, for example, saw Leadership skills, not so much as a set of traits, but as a pattern of motives. He claimed that successful leaders will tend to have a high need for power, a low need for affiliation, and a high level of what he called activity inhibition (one might call it self-control).

Path-goal theory

The path-goal theory is a leadership theory in the field of organizational studies developed by Robert House, an Ohio State University graduate, in 1971 and revised in 1996. The theory states that a leader`s behavior is contingent to the satisfaction, motivation and performance of his subordinates. The revised version also argues that the leader engages in behaviors that complement subordinate`s abilities and compensate for deficiencies. The path-goal model can be classified both as a contingency or as a transactional leadership theory.

Servant leadership

Servant leadership is a philosophy and practice of leadership, coined and defined by Robert Greenleaf and supported by many leadership and management writers such as James Autry, Ken Blanchard, Stephen Covey, Peter Block, Peter Senge, Max DePree, Larry Spears, Margaret Wheatley, James C. Hunter, Kent Keith, Ken Jennings, Don Frick and others. Servant-leaders achieve results for their organizations by giving priority attention to the needs of their colleagues and those they serve. Servant-leaders are often seen as humble stewards of their organization`s resources.

Absenteeism

Absenteeism is a habitual pattern of absence from a duty or obligation.

Frequent absence from the workplace may be indicative of poor morale or of sick building syndrome. However, many employers have implemented absence policies which make no distinction between absences for genuine illness and absence for inappropriate reasons.

Models

Experience curve re-directs here. For its use in video games see Experience point.
Models of the learning curve effect and the closely related experience curve effect express the relationship between equations for experience and efficiency or between efficiency gains and investment in the effort.

Economic value

The Economic value of a good or service has puzzled economists since the beginning of the discipline. First, economists tried to estimate the value of a good to an individual alone, and extend that definition to goods which can be exchanged. From this analysis came the concepts value in use and value in exchange.Wealth maximization predicts that a person will choose to obtain the good or service in the place where it is cheapest, where the amount given up is the least.Value is linked to price through the mechanism of exchange. When an economist observes an exchange, two important value functions are revealed: those of the buyer and seller. Just as the buyer reveals what he is willing to pay for a certain amount of a good, so too does the seller reveal what it costs him to give up the good.

Tolerance

Toleration and Tolerance are terms used in social, cultural and religious contexts to describe attitudes which are `tolerant` (or moderately respectful) of practices or group memberships that may be disapproved of by those in the majority. In practice, Tolerance indicates support for practices that prohibit ethnic and religious discrimination. Conversely, `in Tolerance ` may be used to refer to the discriminatory practices sought to be prohibited.

Goal

A Goal or objective is a projected state of affairs that a person or a system plans or intends to achieve--a personal or organizational desired end-point in some sort of assumed development. Many people endeavor to reach Goals within a finite time by setting deadlines.
A desire or an intention becomes a Goal if and only if one activates an action for achieving it .

Conflict

Many NGOs and independent groups attempt to monitor the situation of ongoing Conflicts. Unfortunately, the definitions of war, Conflict, armed struggle, revolution and all these words which describe violent opposition between States or armed organised groups, are not precise enough to distinguish one from another. For example, the word terrorism is used indifferently by many governments to delegitimate every kind of armed revolt and, at the same time, by many rebel groups to delegitimate the armed repression of sovereign.

Team

A team comprises a group of people or animals linked in a common purpose. teams are especially appropriate for conducting tasks that are high in complexity and have many interdependent subtasks.

	A group in itself does not necessarily constitute a team.
Group	In business, a group, business group, corporate group) alliance is most commonly a legal entity that is a type of conglomerate or holding company consisting of a parent company and subsidiaries. Typical examples are Adidas group or Icelandair group. In United Arab Emirates, Business group can also be knows as Trade association.
Gaussian adaptation	Gaussian adaptation is an evolutionary algorithm designed for the maximization of manufacturing yield due to statistical deviation of component values of signal processing systems. In short, Gaussian adaptation is a stochastic adaptive process where a number of samples of an n-dimensional vector $x[x^T = (x_1, x_2, .. x_n)]$ are taken from a multivariate Gaussian distribution, N (m, M), having mean m and moment matrix M. The samples are tested for fail or pass. The first- and second-order moments of the Gaussian restricted to the pass samples are m* and M*.
Brain drain	Brain drain or human capital flight is a large emigration of individuals with technical skills or knowledge, normally due to conflict, lack of opportunity, political instability, since emigrants usually take with them the fraction of value of their training sponsored by the government. It is a parallel of capital flight which refers to the same movement of financial capital.
Occupational Safety and Health Act	The Occupational Safety and Health Act is the primary federal law which governs occupational health and safety in the private sector and federal government in the United States. It was enacted by Congress in 1970 and was signed by President Richard Nixon on December 29, 1970. Its main goal is to ensure that employers provide employees with an environment free from recognized hazards, such as exposure to toxic chemicals, excessive noise levels, mechanical dangers, heat or cold stress, or unsanitary conditions. The Act can be found in the United States Code at title 29, chapter 15.
Co-creation	Co-creation is the practice of developing systems, products, companies and customers, or managers and employees. Isaac Newton said that in his great work, he stood on the shoulders of giants. Co-creation could be seen as creating great work by standing together with those for whom the project is intended.
Competition	Co-operative Competition is based upon promoting mutual survival - `everyone wins`. Adam Smith`s `invisible hand` is a process where individuals compete to improve their level of happiness but compete in a cooperative manner through peaceful exchange and without violating other people. Cooperative Competition focuses individuals/groups/organisms against the environment.

Top-Down	Top-down and bottom-up are strategies of information processing and knowledge ordering, mostly involving software, but also other humanistic and scientific theories . In practice, they can be seen as a style of thinking and teaching. In many cases Top-down is used as a synonym of analysis or decomposition, and bottom-up of synthesis.
Checklist	A Checklist is a type of informational job aid used to reduce failure by compensating for potential limits of human memory and attention. It helps to ensure consistency and completeness in carrying out a task. A basic example is the `to do list.` A more advanced Checklist would be a schedule, which lays out tasks to be done according to time of day or other factors.

Emergency	An Emergency is a situation which poses an immediate risk to health, life, property or environment. Most emergencies require urgent intervention to prevent a worsening of the situation, although in some situations, mitigation may not be possible and agencies may only be able to offer palliative care for the aftermath. Whilst some emergencies are self evident (such as a natural disaster which threatens many lives), many smaller incidents require the subjective opinion of an observer (or affected party) in order to decide whether it qualifies as an Emergency.
Customer service	Customer service is the provision of service to customers before, during and after a purchase. According to Jamier L. Scott. (2002), `Customer service is a series of activities designed to enhance the level of customer satisfaction - that is, the feeling that a product or service has met the customer expectation.` Its importance varies by product, industry and customer; defective or broken merchandise can be exchanged, often only with a receipt and within a specified time frame.
Decision making	Decision making can be regarded as the mental processes resulting in the selection of a course of action among several alternatives. Every Decision making process produces a final choice. The output can be an action or an opinion of choice.
Hostile work environment	A Hostile work environment exists when an employee experiences workplace harassment and fears going to work because of the offensive, intimidating, religion, sex, national origin, age, disability, veteran status, or, in some jurisdictions, sexual orientation, political affiliation, citizenship status, marital status, or personal appearance. Hostile work environment is also one of the two legal categories of sexual harassment. A Hostile work environment may also be defined as when a boss or manager begins to engage in a manner designed to make you quit in retaliation for your actions.
Performance management	Performance management includes activities to ensure that goals are consistently being met in an effective and efficient manner. Performance management can focus on the performance of an organization, a department, employee, or even the processes to build a product or service, as well as many other areas.

Probability	Probability is a way of expressing knowledge or belief that an event will occur or has occurred. In mathematics the concept has been given an exact meaning in Probability theory, that is used extensively in such areas of study as mathematics, statistics, finance, gambling, science, and philosophy to draw conclusions about the likelihood of potential events and the underlying mechanics of complex systems.
Probability theory	Probability theory is the branch of mathematics concerned with analysis of random phenomena. The central objects of Probability theory are random variables, stochastic processes, and events: mathematical abstractions of non-deterministic events or measured quantities that may either be single occurrences or evolve over time in an apparently random fashion. Although an individual coin toss or the roll of a die is a random event, if repeated many times the sequence of random events will exhibit certain statistical patterns, which can be studied and predicted.
Decision tree	A Decision tree is a decision support tool that uses a tree-like graph or model of decisions and their possible consequences, including chance event outcomes, resource costs, and utility. Decision trees are commonly used in operations research, specifically in decision analysis, to help identify a strategy most likely to reach a goal. Another use of Decision trees is as a descriptive means for calculating conditional probabilities.
Economic value	The Economic value of a good or service has puzzled economists since the beginning of the discipline. First, economists tried to estimate the value of a good to an individual alone, and extend that definition to goods which can be exchanged. From this analysis came the concepts value in use and value in exchange.Wealth maximization predicts that a person will choose to obtain the good or service in the place where it is cheapest, where the amount given up is the least.Value is linked to price through the mechanism of exchange. When an economist observes an exchange, two important value functions are revealed: those of the buyer and seller. Just as the buyer reveals what he is willing to pay for a certain amount of a good, so too does the seller reveal what it costs him to give up the good.
Single version of the truth	In computerized business management, Single version of the truth is a technical concept describing the data warehousing ideal of having either a single centralised database, or at least a distributed synchronised database, which stores all of an organisation`s data in a consistent and non-redundant form.

	In some systems and in the context of message processing systems (often realtime systems), this term also refers to the goal of establishing a single agreed sequence of messages within a database formed by a particular but arbitrary sequencing of records. The key concept is that data combined in a certain sequence is a `truth` which may be analyzed and processed giving particular results, and that although the sequence is arbitrary (and thus another correct but equally arbitrary sequencing would ultimately provide different results in any analysis), it is desirable to agree that the sequence enshrined in the `Single version of the truth` is the version that will be considered `the truth`, and that any conclusions drawn from analysis of the database are valid and unarguable, and (in a technical context) the database may be duplicated to a backup environment to ensure a persistent record is kept of the `Single version of the truth`.
Group	In business, a group, business group, corporate group) alliance is most commonly a legal entity that is a type of conglomerate or holding company consisting of a parent company and subsidiaries. Typical examples are Adidas group or Icelandair group. In United Arab Emirates, Business group can also be knows as Trade association.
Groups decision making	Groups decision making is decision making in groups consisting of multiple members/entities. The challenge of group decision is taking into consideration the various opinions of the different individuals and deciding what action a group should take. There are various systems designed to solve this problem.
Groupthink	Groupthink is a type of thought within a deeply cohesive in-group whose members try to minimize conflict and reach consensus without critically testing, analyzing, and evaluating ideas. It is a second potential negative consequence of group cohesion. Irving Janis studied a number of American Foreign policy `disasters` such as failure to anticipate the Japanese attack on Pearl Harbor ; the Bay of Pigs fiasco (1961) when the US adminstration sought to overthrow Cuban Government of Fidel Castro; and the prosecution of the Vietnam War (1964-67) by President Lyndon Johnson.
Brainstorming	Brainstorming is a group creativity technique designed to generate a large number of ideas for the solution of a problem. In 1953 the method was popularized by Alex Faickney Osborn in a book called Applied Imagination. Osborn proposed that groups could double their creative output with Brainstorming.

Project Management	Project management is the discipline of planning, organizing, and managing resources to bring about the successful completion of specific project goals and objectives. It is sometimes conflated with program management, however technically a program is actually a higher level construct: a group of related and somehow interdependent projects. A project is a temporary endeavor, having a defined beginning and end (usually constrained by date, but can be by funding or deliverables), undertaken to meet unique goals and objectives, usually to bring about beneficial change or added value.

Xerox	Xerox Corporation is a global document management company which manufactures and sells a range of color and black-and-white printers, multifunction systems, photo copiers, digital production printing presses, and related consulting services and supplies. Xerox is headquartered in Norwalk, Connecticut , though its largest population of employees is based in and around Rochester, New York, the area in which the company was founded. The Xerox 914 was the first one-piece plain paper photocopier, and sold in the thousands. Xerox was founded in 1906 in Rochester, New York as `The Haloid Company`, which originally manufactured photographic paper and equipment.
Feedback	Feedback describes the situation when output from (or information about the result of) an event or phenomenon in the past will influence an occurrence or occurrences of the same (i.e. same defined) event / phenomenon in the present or future. When an event is part of a chain of cause-and-effect that forms a circuit or loop, then the event is said to `feed back` into itself.
Performance appraisal	A Performance appraisal is a method by which the job performance of an employee is evaluated (generally in terms of quality, quantity, cost, and time) typically by the corresponding manager or supervisor. A Performance appraisal is a part of guiding and managing career development. It is the process of obtaining, analyzing, and recording information about the relative worth of an employee to the organization.
Active listening	Active listening is a communication technique. Active listening requires the listener to understand, interpret, and evaluate what they hear. The ability to listen actively can improve personal relationships through reducing conflicts, strengthening cooperation, and fostering understanding.
Information overload	Information overload is a term popularized by Alvin Toffler that refers to the difficulty a person can have understanding an issue and making decisions that can be caused by the presence of too much information. The term itself is mentioned in a 1964 book by Bertram Gross, The Managing of Organizations.
Choice	Choice consists of the mental process of judging the merits of multiple options and selecting one of them. While a Choice can be made between imagined options (`what would I do if ...?`), often a Choice is made between real options, and followed by the corresponding action. For example, a route for a journey is chosen based on the preference of arriving at a given destination as soon as possible.
Nonverbal	Nonverbal communications (NVC) is usually understood as the process of communication through sending and receiving wordless messages.

	NVC can be communicated through gesture and touch (Haptic communication), by body language or posture, by facial expression and eye contact. NVC can be communicated through object communication such as clothing, hairstyles or even architecture, symbols and infographics.
Nonverbal communication	Nonverbal communication is usually understood as the process of communication through sending and receiving wordless messages. i.e., language is not the only source of communication, there are other means also. NVC can be communicated through gestures and touch (Haptic communication), by body language or posture, by facial expression and eye contact.
Case study	A Case study is one of several ways of doing research whether it is social science related or even socially related. It is an intensive study of a single group, incident, or community. Other ways include experiments, surveys, or analysis of archival information.
Generalized additive model	In statistics, the Generalized additive model is a statistical model developed by Trevor Hastie and Rob Tibshirani for blending properties of generalized linear models with additive models. The model specifies a distribution (such as a normal distribution, or a binomial distribution) and a link function g relating the expected value of the distribution to the predictors, and attempts to fit functions f_i to satisfy: $$g(\mathrm{E}(Y)) = \beta_0 + f_1(x_1) + f_2(x_2) + \cdots + f_m(x_m).$$ The functions $f_i(x_i)$ may be fit using parametric or non-parametric means, thus providing the potential for better fits to data than other methods. The method hence is very general - a typical Generalized additive model might use a scatterplot smoothing function such as a locally weighted mean for $f_1(x_1)$, and then use a factor model for $f_2(x_2)$. By allowing nonparametric fits, well designed Generalized additive models allow good fits to the training data with relaxed assumptions on the actual relationship, perhaps at the expense of interpretability of results.
Lateral communication	In organizations and organisms, lateral communication works in contrast to traditional top-down, bottom-up or hierarchic communication and involves the spreading of messages from individuals across the base of a pyramid.

lateral communication in organism or animals can give rise to Collective intelligence, or the appearance of Collective intelligence.

Examples of lateral communication in organisms include:

· A coordinated flock of birds or a shoal of fish all maintain their relative positions, or alter direction simultaneously due to lateral communication amongst members; this is achieved due to tiny pressure variations.

· An ants, termites, bees nest is not coordinated by messages sent by the queen ant / bee / termite but by the lateral communication, mediated by scent trails of the ants. Its physical structure is an emergent property of the individual entities.

· Bacterial colonies communicate with each other, coordinating for example an attack, or the product in of slime using lateral communication based on chemical messengers so that as a group they can detect how many colleagues there are, and if they are likely to overwhelm a target.

· The pacemaker cells in the heart, Cardiac pacemaker is a very small group of cells, where lateral communications sweeps through the cells, much like a Mexican wave as a three dimensional circulating wave, which relays contraction signals to the whole heart.

· With Slime mold millions of individual amoeba like creatures can spread out and graze the surface of a leaf.

Upward communication

Upward communication is the process of information flowing from the lower levels of a hierarchy to the upper levels. This type of communication is becoming more and more popular in organizations as traditional forms of communication are becoming less popular. The more traditional organization types such as a hierarchy, places people into separate ranks.

Chapter 11. Motivating Employees

Motivation	Motivation is the activation or energization of goal-oriented behavior. Motivation may be internal or external. The term is generally used for humans but, theoretically, it can also be used to describe the causes for animal behavior as well.
Customer service	Customer service is the provision of service to customers before, during and after a purchase. According to Jamier L. Scott. (2002), `Customer service is a series of activities designed to enhance the level of customer satisfaction - that is, the feeling that a product or service has met the customer expectation.` Its importance varies by product, industry and customer; defective or broken merchandise can be exchanged, often only with a receipt and within a specified time frame.
Needs assessment	Needs assessment is practically ubiquitous today among planners and designers, often identified as the first step in any planning or design process. Over the past four decades, there has been a proliferation of models for Needs assessment with dozens of models to choose from. What nearly all models share is a definition of Needs assessment as identification of a `gap` - but a gap in what differs from model to model.
Group	In business, a group, business group, corporate group) alliance is most commonly a legal entity that is a type of conglomerate or holding company consisting of a parent company and subsidiaries. Typical examples are Adidas group or Icelandair group. In United Arab Emirates, Business group can also be knows as Trade association.
Flextime	Flextime is a variable work schedule, in contrast to traditional work arrangements requiring employees to work a standard 9am to 5pm day. Its invention is usually credited to William Henning. Under Flextime, there is typically a core period of the day when employees are expected to be at work (for example, between 11 am and 3pm), while the rest of the working day is `flexitime`, in which employees can choose when they work, subject to achieving total daily, weekly or monthly hours in the region of what the employer expects, and subject to the necessary work being done.
Job sharing	Job sharing is an employment arrangement where typically two people are retained on a part-time or reduced-time basis to perform a job normally fulfilled by one person working full-time. Compensation is apportioned between the workers, thus leading to a net reduction in per-employee income. Job sharing should not be confused with the more pejorative term featherbedding, which describes the deliberate retention of excess workers on a payroll.

Part-time	A part-time job is a form of employment that carries fewer hours per week than a full-time job. Workers are considered to be part-time if they commonly work fewer than 30 or 35 hours per week. According to the International Labour Organization, the number of part-time workers has increased from one-fourth to a half in the past 20 years in most developed countries, excluding the United States.
Telecommuting	Telecommuting, e-commuting, e-work, telework, working from home (WFH)) is a work arrangement in which employees enjoy flexibility in working location and hours. In other words, the daily commute to a central place of work is replaced by telecommunication links. Many work from home, while others, occasionally also referred to as nomad workers or web commuters utilize mobile telecommunications technology to work from coffee shops or myriad other locations.
Response surface methodology	In statistics, Response surface methodology explores the relationships between several explanatory variables and one or more response variables. The method was introduced by G. E. P. Box and K. B. Wilson in 1951. The main idea of Response surface methodology is to use a sequence of designed experiments to obtain an optimal response. Box and Wilson suggest using a second-degree polynomial model to do this. They acknowledge that this model is only an approximation, but use it because such a model is easy to estimate and apply, even when little is known about the process.
Hygiene factors	Hygiene factors are job factors that can cause dissatisfaction if missing but do not necessarily motivate employees if increased. Hygiene factors have mostly to do with the job environment. These factors are important or notable only when they are lacking.
Two-factor theory	The Two-factor theory states that there are certain factors in the workplace that cause job satisfaction, while a separate set of factors cause dissatisfaction. It was developed by Frederick Herzberg, a psychologist, who theorized that job satisfaction and job dissatisfaction act independently of each other. Attitudes and their connection with industrial mental health are related to Maslow`s theory of motivation.

Turnover	In a human resources context, Turnover is the rate at which an employer gains and loses employees. Simple ways to describe it are `how long employees tend to stay` or `the rate of traffic through the revolving door.` Turnover is measured for individual companies and for their industry as a whole. If an employer is said to have a high Turnover relative to its competitors, it means that employees of that company have a shorter average tenure than those of other companies in the same industry.
Behavior modification	Behavior modification is the use of empirically demonstrated behavior change techniques to improve behavior, such as altering an individual`s behaviors and reactions to stimuli through positive and negative reinforcement of adaptive behavior and/or the reduction of maladaptive behavior through its extinction, punishment and/or therapy.
Family and Medical Leave Act of 1993	The Family and Medical Leave Act of 1993 was signed into law on 5 February 1993 by President Bill Clinton . However, it did not take effect until August 5, 1993: a full six months after the president`s signature. The bill was among the first signed into law by President Clinton in his first term.
Incentive	In economics and sociology, an Incentive is any factor (financial or non-financial) that enables or motivates a particular course of action, the study of Incentive structures is central to the study of all economic activity (both in terms of individual decision-making and in terms of co-operation and competition within a larger institutional structure).
Substance abuse	Substance abuse refers to a maladaptive pattern of use of a substance that is not considered dependent. The term `drug abuse` does not exclude dependency, but is otherwise used in a similar manner in nonmedical contexts. The terms have a huge range of definitions related to taking a psychoactive drug or performance enhancing drug for a non-therapeutic or non-medical effect.
Theory X	Theory x is a theory of human motivation created and developed by Douglas McGregor at the MIT Sloan School of Management in the 1960s that has been used in human resource management, organizational behavior, organizational communication and organizational development. In Theory x, which many managers practice, management assumes employees are inherently lazy and will avoid work if they can. They inherently dislike work. Because of this, workers need to be closely supervised and comprehensive systems of controls developed.

Chapter 11. Motivating Employees

Theory X and Theory Y	Theory X and theory Y are theories of human motivation created and developed by Douglas McGregor at the MIT Sloan School of Management in the 1960s that have been used in human resource management, organizational behavior, organizational communication and organizational development. They describe two very different attitudes toward workforce motivation. McGregor felt that companies followed either one or the other approach.
Wage	A Wage is a compensation, usually financial, received by a worker in exchange for their labor. Compensation in terms of Wage s is given to worker and compensation in terms of salary is given to employees. Compensation is a monetary benefits given to employees in returns of the services provided by them.
Cross-training	Cross-training refers to training in different ways to improve overall performance. It takes advantage of the particular effectiveness of each training method, while at the same time attempting to neglect the shortcomings of that method by combining it with other methods that address its weaknesses. With respect to employee-employer relationship, Cross-training refers to the training of one employee to do another`s work.
Job enlargement	Job enlargement means increasing the scope of a job through extending the range of its job duties and responsibilities. This contradicts the principles of specialisation and the division of labour whereby work is divided into small units, each of which is performed repetitively by an individual worker. Some motivational theories suggest that the boredom and alienation caused by the division of labour can actually cause efficiency to fall.
Job enrichment	Job enrichment is an attempt to motivate employees by giving them the opportunity to use the range of their abilities. It is an idea that was developed by the American psychologist Frederick Herzberg in the 1950s. It can be contrasted to job enlargement which simply increases the number of tasks without changing the challenge.
Job rotation	Job rotation is an approach to management development where an individual is moved through a schedule of assignments designed to give him or her a breadth of exposure to the entire operation. Job rotation is also practiced to allow qualified employees to gain more insights into the processes of a company, and to reduce boredom and increase job satisfaction through job variation.

The term Job rotation can also mean the scheduled exchange of persons in offices, especially in public offices, prior to the end of incumbency or the legislative period.

Theory Z

Theory Z is a name applied to three distinctly different psychological theories. One was developed by Abraham H. Maslow in his paper Theory Z and the other is Dr. William Ouchi`s so-called `Japanese Management` style popularized during the Asian economic boom of the 1980s. The third was developed by W. J. Reddin in Managerial Effectiveness.
Maslow`s Theory Z` In contrast to Theory X, which stated that workers inherently dislike and avoid work and must be driven to it, and Theory Y, which stated that work is natural and can be a source of satisfaction when aimed at higher order human psychological needs.

For Ouchi, Theory Z focused on increasing employee loyalty to the company by providing a job for life with a strong focus on the well-being of the employee, both on and off the job. According to Ouchi, Theory Z management tends to promote stable employment, high productivity, and high employee morale and satisfaction.

Pygmalion effect

The Pygmalion effect refers to the phenomenon in which the greater the expectation placed upon people, often children or students and employees, the better they perform. The effect is named after Pygmalion, a Cypriot sculptor in a narrative by Ovid in Greek mythology, who fell in love with a female statue he had carved out of ivory.

The Pygmalion effect is a form of self-fulfilling prophecy, and, in this respect, people with poor expectations internalize their negative label, and those with positive labels succeed accordingly.

Management by objectives

Management by objectives is a process of agreeing upon objectives within an organization so that management and employees agree to the objectives and understand what they are in the organization.

The term `Management by objectives` was first popularized by Peter Drucker in his 1954 book `The Practice of Management`.

The essence of Management by objectives is participative goal setting, choosing course of actions and decision making. An important part of the Management by objectives is the measurement and the comparison of the employee`s actual performance with the standards set. Ideally, when employees themselves have been involved with the goal setting and choosing the course of action to be followed by them, they are more likely to fulfill their responsibilities.

Market	A Market is any one of a variety of different systems, institutions, procedures, social relations and infrastructures whereby persons trade, and goods and services are exchanged, forming part of the economy. It is an arrangement that allows buyers and sellers to exchange things. Markets vary in size, range, geographic scale, location, types and variety of human communities, as well as the types of goods and services traded.
Absenteeism	Absenteeism is a habitual pattern of absence from a duty or obligation. Frequent absence from the workplace may be indicative of poor morale or of sick building syndrome. However, many employers have implemented absence policies which make no distinction between absences for genuine illness and absence for inappropriate reasons.
Decision making	Decision making can be regarded as the mental processes resulting in the selection of a course of action among several alternatives. Every Decision making process produces a final choice. The output can be an action or an opinion of choice.
Groups decision making	Groups decision making is decision making in groups consisting of multiple members/entities. The challenge of group decision is taking into consideration the various opinions of the different individuals and deciding what action a group should take. There are various systems designed to solve this problem.
Feedback	Feedback describes the situation when output from (or information about the result of) an event or phenomenon in the past will influence an occurrence or occurrences of the same (i.e. same defined) event / phenomenon in the present or future. When an event is part of a chain of cause-and-effect that forms a circuit or loop, then the event is said to `feed back` into itself.
Performance appraisal	A Performance appraisal is a method by which the job performance of an employee is evaluated (generally in terms of quality, quantity, cost, and time) typically by the corresponding manager or supervisor. A Performance appraisal is a part of guiding and managing career development. It is the process of obtaining, analyzing, and recording information about the relative worth of an employee to the organization.

Absenteeism	Absenteeism is a habitual pattern of absence from a duty or obligation. Frequent absence from the workplace may be indicative of poor morale or of sick building syndrome. However, many employers have implemented absence policies which make no distinction between absences for genuine illness and absence for inappropriate reasons.
Reduce	For example, it is fairly easy for a top executive to reduce the price of his/her company`s stock - due to information asymmetry. The executive can accelerate accounting of expected expenses, delay accounting of expected revenue, engage in off balance sheet transactions to make the company`s profitability appear temporarily poorer, or simply promote and report severely conservative (eg. pessimistic) estimates of future earnings.
Substance abuse	Substance abuse refers to a maladaptive pattern of use of a substance that is not considered dependent. The term `drug abuse` does not exclude dependency, but is otherwise used in a similar manner in nonmedical contexts. The terms have a huge range of definitions related to taking a psychoactive drug or performance enhancing drug for a non-therapeutic or non-medical effect.
Drug test	A Drug test is a technical analysis of a biological specimen - urine, hair, blood, sweat, federal mandated and general workplace. Federal mandated Drug testing started when President Ronald Reagan enacted via executive order, that federal workers refrain from using illegal substances.
Workplace violence	Workplace violence refers to violence that originates from employees or employers and threatens employers and/or other employees. The definition of work related violence that has received pan-European acceptance is as follows: `incidents where people are abused, threatened or assaulted in circumstances relating to their work, involving an explicit or implicit challenge to their safety, well-being or health`. This can involve violence resulting from industrial disputes, although this is not a major factor in most incidents.
Fraud	In the broadest sense, a Fraud is an intentional deception made for personal gain or to damage another individual. The specific legal definition varies by legal jurisdiction. Fraud is a crime, and is also a civil law violation.

Background check	A Background check or background investigation is the process of looking up and compiling criminal records, commercial records and financial records (in certain instances such as employment screening) of an individual. Background checks are often requested by employers on job candidates, especially on candidates seeking a position that requires high security or a position of trust, such as in a school, hospital, financial institution, airport, and government. These checks are traditionally administered by a government agency for a nominal fee, but can also be administered by private companies.
HealthCare	Healthcare is rationed in the United States in various ways. Access to private health care insurance is rationed in part on price and ability to pay. Those not able to afford a health insurance policy are unable to acquire one, and sometimes insurance companies pre-screen applicants for pre-existing medical conditions and either decline to cover the applicant or apply additional price and medical coverage conditions.
Evaluation	Evaluation is systematic determination of merit, worth, and significance of something or someone using criteria against a set of standards. Evaluation often is used to characterize and appraise subjects of interest in a wide range of human enterprises, including the arts, criminal justice, foundations and non-profit organizations, government, health care, and other human services.
Employee assistance	Employee assistance Programs (EAPs) are employee benefit programs offered by many employers, typically in conjunction with a health insurance plan. EAPs are intended to help employees deal with personal problems that might adversely impact their work performance, health, and well-being. EAPs generally include assessment, short-term counseling and referral services for employees and their household members.
Employee assistance programs	Employee assistance programs are employee benefit programs offered by many employers, typically in conjunction with a health insurance plan. Employee assistance programs are intended to help employees deal with personal problems that might adversely impact their work performance, health, and well-being. Employee assistance programss generally include assessment, short-term counseling and referral services for employees and their household members.

Small Business	A small business is a business that is privately owned and operated, with a small number of employees and relatively low volume of sales. The legal definition of `small` often varies by country and industry, but is generally under 100 employees in the United States and under 50 employees in the European Union. In comparison, the definition of mid-sized business by the number of employees is generally under 500 in the U.S. and 250 for the European Union.
Small Business Administration	The Small Business Administration is a United States government agency that provides support to small businesses. The mission of the Small Business Administration is `to maintain and strengthen the nation`s economy by enabling the establishment and viability of small businesses and by assisting in the economic recovery of communities after disasters.` The Small Business Administration makes loans directly to businesses and acts as a guarantor on bank loans. In some circumstances it also makes loans to victims of natural disasters, works to get government procurement contracts for small businesses, and assists businesses with management, technical and training issues.
Procedure	A procedure is a specified series of actions or operations which have to be executed in the same manner in order to always obtain the same result under the same circumstances (for example, emergency procedures). Less precisely speaking, this word can indicate a sequence of activities, tasks, steps, decisions, calculations and processes, that when undertaken in the sequence laid down produces the described result, product or outcome. A procedure usually induces a change.

Time management	Time management refers to a range of skills, tools, and techniques used to manage time when accomplishing specific tasks, projects and goals. This set encompasses a wide scope of activities, and these include planning, allocating, setting goals, delegation, analysis of time spent, monitoring, organizing, scheduling, and prioritizing. Initially Time management referred to just business or work activities, but eventually the term broadened to include personal activities as well.
Planning	Planning in organizations and public policy is both the organizational process of creating and maintaining a plan; and the psychological process of thinking about the activities required to create a desired goal on some scale. As such, it is a fundamental property of intelligent behavior. This thought process is essential to the creation and refinement of a plan, or integration of it with other plans, that is, it combines forecasting of developments with the preparation of scenarios of how to react to them.
Brown	Brown is a color term, denoting a range of composite colors produced by a mixture of orange, red or yellow with black. The term is from Old English brún, in origin for any dusky or dark shade of color. The Common Germanic adjective *brûnoz, *brûnâ meant both dark colors and a glistening or shining quality, whence burnish.
Process analytical technology	Process analytical technology has been defined by the United States Food and Drug Administration (FDA) as a mechanism to design, analyze, and control pharmaceutical manufacturing processes through the measurement of Critical Process Parameters (CPP) which affect Critical Quality Attributes (CQA). The concept actually aims at understanding the processes by defining their CPP`s, and accordingly monitoring them in a timely manner (preferably in-line or on-line) and thus being more efficient in testing while at the same time reducing over-processing, enhancing consistency and minimizing rejects.
Case study	A Case study is one of several ways of doing research whether it is social science related or even socially related. It is an intensive study of a single group, incident, or community. Other ways include experiments, surveys, or analysis of archival information.
Delegation	Delegation is the assignment of authority and responsibility to another person to carry out specific activities. However the person who delegated the work remains accountable for the outcome of the delegated work. delegation empowers a subordinate to make decisions, i.e. it is a shift of decision-making authority from one organizational level to a lower one.
Absenteeism	Absenteeism is a habitual pattern of absence from a duty or obligation.

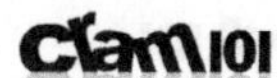

	Frequent absence from the workplace may be indicative of poor morale or of sick building syndrome. However, many employers have implemented absence policies which make no distinction between absences for genuine illness and absence for inappropriate reasons.
Career	Career is a term defined by the Oxford English Dictionary as an individual`s `course or progress through life `. It is usually considered to pertain to remunerative work (and sometimes also formal education). The etymology of the term is somewhat ironic in that it comes from the Latin word carrera, which means race .
Conflict	Many NGOs and independent groups attempt to monitor the situation of ongoing Conflicts. Unfortunately, the definitions of war, Conflict, armed struggle, revolution and all these words which describe violent opposition between States or armed organised groups, are not precise enough to distinguish one from another. For example, the word terrorism is used indifferently by many governments to delegitimate every kind of armed revolt and, at the same time, by many rebel groups to delegitimate the armed repression of sovereign.
Work-family Conflict	Work-family conflict is `a form of interrole conflict in which the role pressures from the work and family domains are mutually incompatible in some respect. That is participation in the work (family) role is made more difficult by virtue of participation in the family (work) role` (Greenhaus ' Beutell, 1985, p.77.) Conflict between work and family is important for organizations and individuals because it is linked to negative consequences.
Reduce	For example, it is fairly easy for a top executive to reduce the price of his/her company`s stock - due to information asymmetry. The executive can accelerate accounting of expected expenses, delay accounting of expected revenue, engage in off balance sheet transactions to make the company`s profitability appear temporarily poorer, or simply promote and report severely conservative (eg. pessimistic) estimates of future earnings.
Hostile work environment	A Hostile work environment exists when an employee experiences workplace harassment and fears going to work because of the offensive, intimidating, religion, sex, national origin, age, disability, veteran status, or, in some jurisdictions, sexual orientation, political affiliation, citizenship status, marital status, or personal appearance. Hostile work environment is also one of the two legal categories of sexual harassment. A Hostile work environment may also be defined as when a boss or manager begins to engage in a manner designed to make you quit in retaliation for your actions.

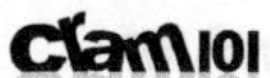

Healthcare	Healthcare is rationed in the United States in various ways. Access to private health care insurance is rationed in part on price and ability to pay. Those not able to afford a health insurance policy are unable to acquire one, and sometimes insurance companies pre-screen applicants for pre-existing medical conditions and either decline to cover the applicant or apply additional price and medical coverage conditions.

Chapter 14. Managing Conflict and Change

Conflict	Many NGOs and independent groups attempt to monitor the situation of ongoing Conflicts. Unfortunately, the definitions of war, Conflict, armed struggle, revolution and all these words which describe violent opposition between States or armed organised groups, are not precise enough to distinguish one from another. For example, the word terrorism is used indifferently by many governments to delegitimate every kind of armed revolt and, at the same time, by many rebel groups to delegitimate the armed repression of sovereign.
Intrapersonal	Intrapersonal communication is language use or thought internal to the communicator. intrapersonal communication is the active internal involvement of the individual in symbolic processing of messages. intrapersonal communication is the thought process or communication with one person or one`s self.
Employment discrimination	Employment discrimination is discrimination in hiring, promotion, job assignment, termination, and compensation. It includes various types of harassment. Many jurisdictions prohibit some types of Employment discrimination, often by forbidding discrimination based on certain traits (`protected categories`).
Conflict management	Conflict management refers to the long-term management of intractable conflicts. It is the label for the variety of ways by which people handle grievances--standing up for what they consider to be right and against what they consider to be wrong. Those ways include such diverse phenomena as gossip, ridicule, lynching, terrorism, warfare, feuding, genocide, law, mediation, and avoidance.
Conflict resolution	Conflict resolution is a range of methods for alleviating or eliminating sources of conflict. The term Conflict resolution is sometimes used interchangeably with the term dispute resolution or alternative dispute resolution. Processes of Conflict resolution generally include negotiation, mediation, and diplomacy.
Timothy	Timothy was a first-century Christian bishop who died about AD 80. Evidence from the New Testament also has him functioning as coadjutor of Saint Paul. Timothy is mentioned in the Bible at the time of Paul`s second visit to Lystra, where Timothy is mentioned as a `disciple`. Paul, having been impressed by his `own son in the faith,` arranged that he should become his companion, and personally circumcised him because his mother was of the Jewish faith, so that he might be accepted by the Jews.

Team	A team comprises a group of people or animals linked in a common purpose. teams are especially appropriate for conducting tasks that are high in complexity and have many interdependent subtasks. A group in itself does not necessarily constitute a team.
Mediation	Mediation, a form of alternative dispute resolution (ADR), is a way of resolving disputes between two or more parties. A third party, the mediator, assists the parties to negotiate their own settlement (facilitative Mediation). In some cases, mediators may express a view on what might be a fair or reasonable settlement, generally where all the parties agree that the mediator may do so (evaluative Mediation).
Artificial neural network	An Artificial neural network is a mathematical model or computational model that tries to simulate the structure and/or functional aspects of biological neural networks. It consists of an interconnected group of artificial neurons and processes information using a connectionist approach to computation. In most cases an Artificial neural network is an adaptive system that changes its structure based on external or internal information that flows through the network during the learning phase.
Innovation	Innovation is a change in the thought process for doing something or `new stuff that is made useful`. It may refer to an incremental emergent or radical and revolutionary changes in thinking, products, processes, or organizations. Following Schumpeter (1934), contributors to the scholarly literature on Innovation typically distinguish between invention, an idea made manifest, and Innovation, ideas applied successfully in practice.
Hostile work environment	A Hostile work environment exists when an employee experiences workplace harassment and fears going to work because of the offensive, intimidating, religion, sex, national origin, age, disability, veteran status, or, in some jurisdictions, sexual orientation, political affiliation, citizenship status, marital status, or personal appearance. Hostile work environment is also one of the two legal categories of sexual harassment. A Hostile work environment may also be defined as when a boss or manager begins to engage in a manner designed to make you quit in retaliation for your actions.
Politics	Politics is a process by which groups of people make collective decisions. The term is generally applied to behavior within civil governments, but Politics has been observed in other group interactions, including corporate, academic, and religious institutions. It consists of `social relations involving authority or power` and refers to the regulation of a political unit, and to the methods and tactics used to formulate and apply policy.

Referent power	Referent power is individual power based on a high level of identification with, admiration of, or respect for the powerholder. Nationalism, patriotism, celebrities and well-respected people are examples of Referent power in effect. Referent power is one of the Five Bases of Social Power, as defined by Bertram Raven and his colleagues in 1959.
Impression management	In sociology and social psychology, Impression management is a goal-directed conscious or unconscious process in which people attempt to influence the perceptions of other people about a person, object or event; they do so by regulating and controlling information in social interaction . It is usually used synonymously with self-presentation, in which a person tries to influence the perception of their image. The notion of Impression management also refers to practices in professional communication and public relations, where the term is used to describe the process of formation of a company`s or organization`s public image.
Absenteeism	Absenteeism is a habitual pattern of absence from a duty or obligation. Frequent absence from the workplace may be indicative of poor morale or of sick building syndrome. However, many employers have implemented absence policies which make no distinction between absences for genuine illness and absence for inappropriate reasons.

Job description	A Job description is a list of the general tasks, or functions, and responsibilities of a position. Typically, it also includes to whom the position reports, specifications such as the qualifications needed by the person in the job, salary range for the position, etc. A Job description is usually developed by conducting a job analysis, which includes examining the tasks and sequences of tasks necessary to perform the job.
Specification	A Specification is an explicit set of requirements to be satisfied by a material, product, or service. Should a material, product or service fail to meet one or more of the applicable Specifications, it may be referred to as being out of specificiation; the abbreviation OOS may also be used. A technical Specification may be developed privately, for example by a corporation, regulatory body, military, etc: It is usually under the umbrella of a quality management system.
Employment	Employment is a contract between two parties, one being the employer and the other being the employee. An employee may be defined as: \`A person in the service of another under any contract of hire, express or implied, oral or written, where the employer has the power or right to control and direct the employee in the material details of how the work is to be performed.\` Black\`s Law Dictionary page 471 (5th ed. 1979). In a commercial setting, the employer conceives of a productive activity, generally with the intention of generating a profit, and the employee contributes labour to the enterprise, usually in return for payment of wages.
Recruitment	\`Onboarding\` is a term which describes the introduction or \`induction\` process. A well-planned introduction helps new employees become fully operational quickly and is often integrated with a new company and environment. Onboarding is included in the Recruitment process for retention purposes.
Healthcare	Healthcare is rationed in the United States in various ways. Access to private health care insurance is rationed in part on price and ability to pay. Those not able to afford a health insurance policy are unable to acquire one, and sometimes insurance companies pre-screen applicants for pre-existing medical conditions and either decline to cover the applicant or apply additional price and medical coverage conditions.
Team	A team comprises a group of people or animals linked in a common purpose. teams are especially appropriate for conducting tasks that are high in complexity and have many interdependent subtasks. A group in itself does not necessarily constitute a team.
Customer service	Customer service is the provision of service to customers before, during and after a purchase.

According to Jamier L. Scott. (2002), `Customer service is a series of activities designed to enhance the level of customer satisfaction - that is, the feeling that a product or service has met the customer expectation.`

Its importance varies by product, industry and customer; defective or broken merchandise can be exchanged, often only with a receipt and within a specified time frame.

Artificial neural network

An Artificial neural network is a mathematical model or computational model that tries to simulate the structure and/or functional aspects of biological neural networks. It consists of an interconnected group of artificial neurons and processes information using a connectionist approach to computation. In most cases an Artificial neural network is an adaptive system that changes its structure based on external or internal information that flows through the network during the learning phase.

Closed-ended question

A Closed-ended question is a form of question which can normally be answered using a simple `yes` or `no`, a specific simple piece of information, or a selection from multiple choices.

Examples include:

· Question: Do you know your weight?

Answer: Yes.

· Question: What is your weight?

Answer: 167 lbs.

Close-ended questions can be used for clarifiying facts, verifying information already given or controlling a conversation, among other things.

Examples of Closed-ended questions:

· Do you get along with your supervisor?

· Is that a photograph of your children?

· Are you leaving right at 5:00 today?

· Are you awake?

A Closed-ended question contrasts with an open-ended question, which cannot be answered with a simple `yes` or `no`, or with a specific piece of information, and which give the person answering the question scope to give the information that seems to them to be appropriate. Open-ended questions are sometimes phrased as a statement which requires a response.

Examples of open-ended questions:

· Tell me about your relationship with your supervisor

· How do you see your future?

· Tell me about the children in this photograph

· What is the purpose of government?

· Why did you choose that answer?

At the same time, there are close-ended questions which are sometimes impossible to answer correctly with a yes or no without confusion, for example: `have you stopped taking heroin?` (if you never took it), see `Loaded question`.

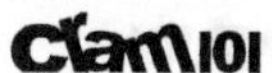

Open-ended question	A closed-ended question is a form of question which can normally be answered using a simple `yes` or `no`, a specific simple piece of information, verifying information already given or controlling a conversation, among other things. A closed-ended question contrasts with an open-ended question, which cannot be answered with a simple `yes` or `no`, or with a specific piece of information, and which give the person answering the question scope to give the information that seems to them to be appropriate. Examples: · What do you think about your weight? · What is the purpose of government? · What is the most important purpose of government? · Why did you choose that answer? At the same time, there are close-ended questions which are sometimes impossible to answer correctly with a yes or no without confusion, for example: `have you stopped taking heroin?` (if you never took it), see `Loaded question`.
Unstructured interviews	Unstructured interviews are a method of interviews where questions can be changed or adapted to meet the respondent`s intelligence, understanding or belief. Unlike a structured interview they do not offer a limited, pre-set range of answers for a respondent to choose, but instead advocate listening to how each individual person responds to the question. The method to gather information using this technique is fairly limited, for example most surveys that are carried out via telephone or even in person tend to follow a structured method.
Halo effect	The Halo effect is a cognitive bias whereby the perception of one trait is influenced by the perception of another trait (or several traits) of that person or object. An example would be judging a good-looking person as more intelligent.

Halo effects happen especially if the perceiver does not have enough information about all traits, so that he makes assumptions based on one or two prominent traits--these one or two prominent traits `overshadow` other traits, similar to the radiation of light in optical Halo effects or halos in iconography (rings of light around someone`s head).

Background check

A Background check or background investigation is the process of looking up and compiling criminal records, commercial records and financial records (in certain instances such as employment screening) of an individual.

Background checks are often requested by employers on job candidates, especially on candidates seeking a position that requires high security or a position of trust, such as in a school, hospital, financial institution, airport, and government. These checks are traditionally administered by a government agency for a nominal fee, but can also be administered by private companies.

Drug test

A Drug test is a technical analysis of a biological specimen - urine, hair, blood, sweat, federal mandated and general workplace. Federal mandated Drug testing started when President Ronald Reagan enacted via executive order, that federal workers refrain from using illegal substances.

Group

In business, a group, business group, corporate group) alliance is most commonly a legal entity that is a type of conglomerate or holding company consisting of a parent company and subsidiaries. Typical examples are Adidas group or Icelandair group.
In United Arab Emirates, Business group can also be knows as Trade association.

Rescue

Rescue refers to operations that usually involve the saving of life, or prevention of injury.

Tools used might include search dogs, search and Rescue horses, helicopters, the `Jaws of Life`, and other hydraulic cutting and spreading tools used to extricate individuals from wrecked vehicles. Rescue operations are sometimes supported by special vehicles such as fire department`s or EMS Heavy Rescue vehicle.

Ropes and special devices can reach and remove individuals and animals from difficult locations including:

· Cave Rescue

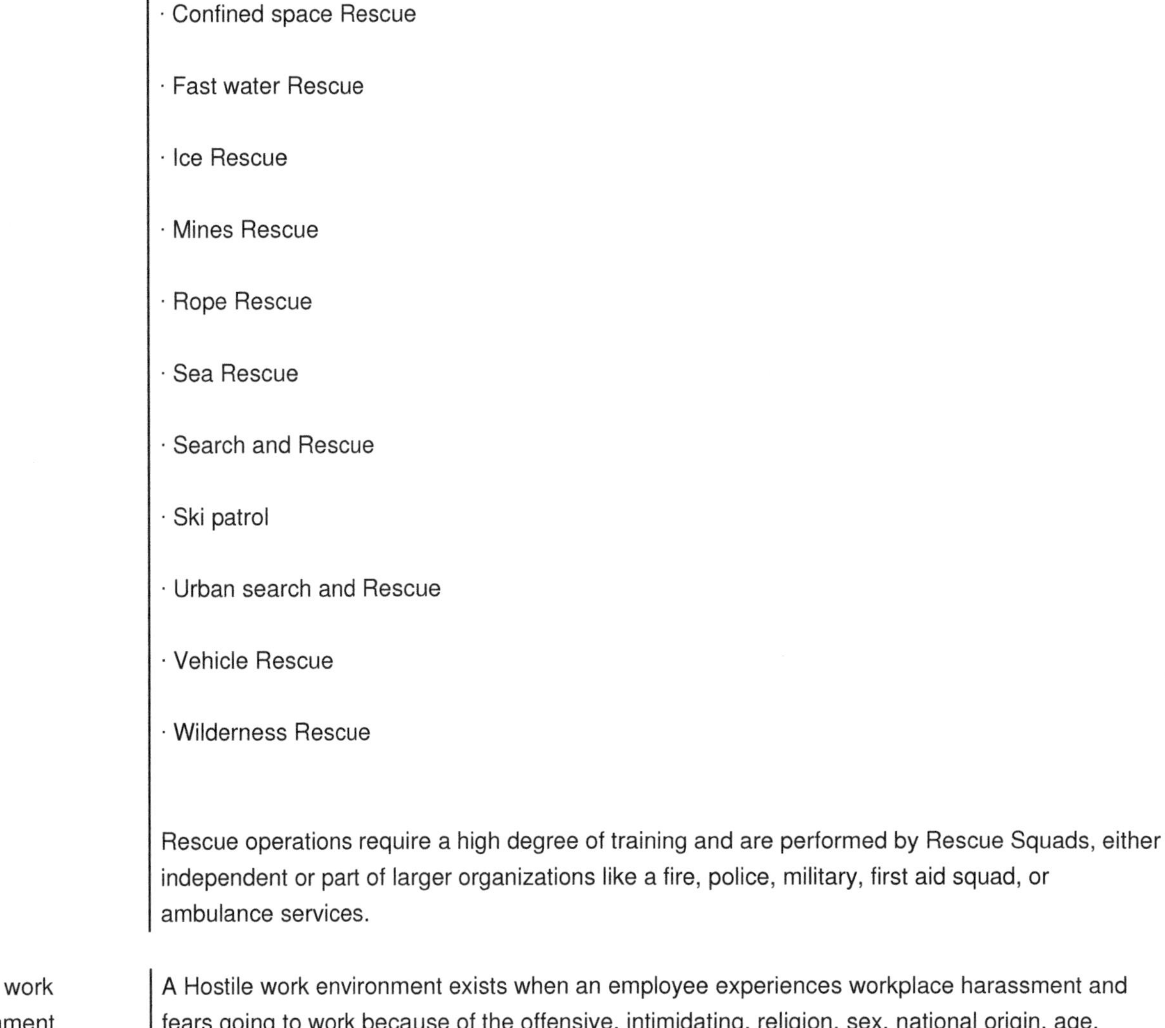

· Confined space Rescue

· Fast water Rescue

· Ice Rescue

· Mines Rescue

· Rope Rescue

· Sea Rescue

· Search and Rescue

· Ski patrol

· Urban search and Rescue

· Vehicle Rescue

· Wilderness Rescue

Rescue operations require a high degree of training and are performed by Rescue Squads, either independent or part of larger organizations like a fire, police, military, first aid squad, or ambulance services.

Hostile work environment

A Hostile work environment exists when an employee experiences workplace harassment and fears going to work because of the offensive, intimidating, religion, sex, national origin, age, disability, veteran status, or, in some jurisdictions, sexual orientation, political affiliation, citizenship status, marital status, or personal appearance. Hostile work environment is also one of the two legal categories of sexual harassment.
A Hostile work environment may also be defined as when a boss or manager begins to engage in a manner designed to make you quit in retaliation for your actions.

Age Discrimination in Employment Act	The Age Discrimination in Employment Act of 1967, Pub. L. No. 90-202, 81 Stat. 602 (Dec. 15, 1967), codified as Chapter 14 of Title 29 of the United States Code, 29 U.S.C. Â§ 621 through 29 U.S.C. Â§ 634 (ADEA), prohibits employment discrimination against persons 40 years of age or older in the United States). The law also sets standards for pensions and benefits provided by employers and requires that information about the needs of older workers be provided to the general public.
Age Discrimination in Employment Act of 1967	The Age Discrimination in Employment Act of 1967, Pub. L. No. 90-202, 81 Stat. 602 (Dec. 15, 1967), codified as Chapter 14 of Title 29 of the United States Code, 29 U.S.C. Â§ 621 through 29 U.S.C. Â§ 634 (ADEA), prohibits employment discrimination against persons 40 years of age or older in the United States). The law also sets standards for pensions and benefits provided by employers and requires that information about the needs of older workers be provided to the general public.
Equal	EQUAL was the `Community Initiative` within the European Social Fund of the European Union. It concerned `transnational co-operation to promote new means of combating all forms of discrimination and inEQUALities in connection with the labour market`. It ran from 2001 till 2007 with a budget of some â,¬3 billion of EU resources, matched by a similar sum from national resources.
Equal Employment Opportunity	The term Equal Employment Opportunity was created by President Lyndon B. Johnson when he signed Executive Order 11246 on September 24, 1965, created to prohibit federal contractors from discriminating against employees on the basis of race, sex, creed, religion, color, or national origin. In more recent times, most employers have also added sexual orientation to the list of non-discrimination. The Executive Order also required contractors to implement affirmative action plans to increase the participation of minorities and women in the workplace.
Equal Employment Opportunity Commission	The U.S. Equal Employment Opportunity Commission is an independent federal agency that enforces laws against workplace discrimination. The Equal Employment Opportunity Commission investigates discrimination complaints based on an individual`s race, color, national origin, religion, sex, sexual orentation, age, disability and retaliation for reporting and/or opposing a discriminatory practice. It is empowered to file discrimination suits against employers on behalf of alleged victims and to adjudicate claims of discrimination brought against federal agencies.

Rehabilitation Act	The U.S. Rehabilitation Act of 1973 prohibits discrimination on the basis of disability in programs conducted by Federal agencies, in programs receiving Federal financial assistance, in Federal employment, and in the employment practices of Federal contractors. The standards for determining employment discrimination under the Rehabilitation Act are the same as those used in title I of the Americans with Disabilities Act.
Affirmative action	Affirmative action refers to policies that take factors including `race, color, religion, sex or national origin` into consideration in order to benefit an underrepresented group, usually as a means to counter the effects of a history of discrimination. The focus of such policies ranges from employment and education to public contracting and health programs. `Affirmative action` is action taken to increase the representation of women and minorities in areas of employment, education, and business from which they have been historically excluded.

United States	The United States of America (commonly referred to as the United States, the U.S., the United StatesA, or America) is a federal constitutional republic comprising fifty states and a federal district. The country is situated mostly in central North America, where its forty-eight contiguous states and Washington, D.C., the capital district, lie between the Pacific and Atlantic Oceans, bordered by Canada to the north and Mexico to the south. The state of Alaska is in the northwest of the continent, with Canada to its east and Russia to the west across the Bering Strait.
Politics	Politics is a process by which groups of people make collective decisions. The term is generally applied to behavior within civil governments, but Politics has been observed in other group interactions, including corporate, academic, and religious institutions. It consists of `social relations involving authority or power` and refers to the regulation of a political unit, and to the methods and tactics used to formulate and apply policy.
Productivity	Productivity is a measure of output from a production process, per unit of input. For example, lab is typically measured as a ratio of output per labor-hour, an input. productivity may be conceived of as a metric of the technical or engineering efficiency of production.
Team	A team comprises a group of people or animals linked in a common purpose. teams are especially appropriate for conducting tasks that are high in complexity and have many interdependent subtasks. A group in itself does not necessarily constitute a team.
Brain drain	Brain drain or human capital flight is a large emigration of individuals with technical skills or knowledge, normally due to conflict, lack of opportunity, political instability, since emigrants usually take with them the fraction of value of their training sponsored by the government. It is a parallel of capital flight which refers to the same movement of financial capital.
Occupational Safety and Health Act	The Occupational Safety and Health Act is the primary federal law which governs occupational health and safety in the private sector and federal government in the United States. It was enacted by Congress in 1970 and was signed by President Richard Nixon on December 29, 1970. Its main goal is to ensure that employers provide employees with an environment free from recognized hazards, such as exposure to toxic chemicals, excessive noise levels, mechanical dangers, heat or cold stress, or unsanitary conditions. The Act can be found in the United States Code at title 29, chapter 15.

Economic value

The Economic value of a good or service has puzzled economists since the beginning of the discipline. First, economists tried to estimate the value of a good to an individual alone, and extend that definition to goods which can be exchanged. From this analysis came the concepts value in use and value in exchange.Wealth maximization predicts that a person will choose to obtain the good or service in the place where it is cheapest, where the amount given up is the least.Value is linked to price through the mechanism of exchange. When an economist observes an exchange, two important value functions are revealed: those of the buyer and seller. Just as the buyer reveals what he is willing to pay for a certain amount of a good, so too does the seller reveal what it costs him to give up the good.

Employee handbook

An Employee handbook details guidelines, expectations and procedures of a business or company to its employees.

Employee handbooks are given to employees on one of the first days of his/her job, in order to acquaint them with their new company and its policies.

While it often varies from business to business, specific areas that an Employee handbook may address include:

· A welcome statement, which may also briefly describe the company`s history, reasons for its success and how the employee can contribute to future successes. It may also include a mission statement, or a statement about a business` goals and objectives.

· Orientation procedures.

Checklist

A Checklist is a type of informational job aid used to reduce failure by compensating for potential limits of human memory and attention. It helps to ensure consistency and completeness in carrying out a task. A basic example is the `to do list.` A more advanced Checklist would be a schedule, which lays out tasks to be done according to time of day or other factors.

Evaluation

Evaluation is systematic determination of merit, worth, and significance of something or someone using criteria against a set of standards. Evaluation often is used to characterize and appraise subjects of interest in a wide range of human enterprises, including the arts, criminal justice, foundations and non-profit organizations, government, health care, and other human services.

Planning	Planning in organizations and public policy is both the organizational process of creating and maintaining a plan; and the psychological process of thinking about the activities required to create a desired goal on some scale. As such, it is a fundamental property of intelligent behavior. This thought process is essential to the creation and refinement of a plan, or integration of it with other plans, that is, it combines forecasting of developments with the preparation of scenarios of how to react to them.
Needs assessment	Needs assessment is practically ubiquitous today among planners and designers, often identified as the first step in any planning or design process. Over the past four decades, there has been a proliferation of models for Needs assessment with dozens of models to choose from. What nearly all models share is a definition of Needs assessment as identification of a `gap` - but a gap in what differs from model to model.
Nominative determinism	Nominative determinism refers to the theory that a person`s name is given an influential role in reflecting key attributes of his job, profession, but real examples are more highly prized, the more obscure the better.
Apprenticeship	Apprenticeship is a system of training a new generation of practitioners of a skill. Apprentices (or in early modern usage `prentices`) or protégés build their careers from apprenticeships. Most of their training is done on the job while working for an employer who helps the apprentices learn their trade, in exchange for their continuing labour for an agreed period after they become skilled.
Cross-training	Cross-training refers to training in different ways to improve overall performance. It takes advantage of the particular effectiveness of each training method, while at the same time attempting to neglect the shortcomings of that method by combining it with other methods that address its weaknesses. With respect to employee-employer relationship, Cross-training refers to the training of one employee to do another`s work.
Group	In business, a group, business group, corporate group) alliance is most commonly a legal entity that is a type of conglomerate or holding company consisting of a parent company and subsidiaries. Typical examples are Adidas group or Icelandair group. In United Arab Emirates, Business group can also be knows as Trade association.

E-learning	E-learning comprises all forms of electronically supported learning and teaching, which are procedural in character and aim to effect the construction of knowledge with reference to individual experience, practice and knowledge of the learner. Information and communication systems, whether networked or not, serve as specific media to implement the learning process. E-learning is essentially the computer and network enabled transfer of skills and knowledge.
Generalized additive model	In statistics, the Generalized additive model is a statistical model developed by Trevor Hastie and Rob Tibshirani for blending properties of generalized linear models with additive models. The model specifies a distribution (such as a normal distribution, or a binomial distribution) and a link function g relating the expected value of the distribution to the predictors, and attempts to fit functions f_i to satisfy: $g(\mathrm{E}(Y)) = \beta_0 + f_1(x_1) + f_2(x_2) + \cdots + f_m(x_m).$ The functions $f_i(x_i)$ may be fit using parametric or non-parametric means, thus providing the potential for better fits to data than other methods. The method hence is very general - a typical Generalized additive model might use a scatterplot smoothing function such as a locally weighted mean for $f_1(x_1)$, and then use a factor model for $f_2(x_2)$. By allowing nonparametric fits, well designed Generalized additive models allow good fits to the training data with relaxed assumptions on the actual relationship, perhaps at the expense of interpretability of results.
Plants	Plants are living organisms belonging to the kingdom Plantae. They include familiar organisms such as trees, herbs, bushes, grasses, vines, ferns, mosses, and green algae. The scientific study of plants, known as botany, has identified about 350,000 extant species of plants, defined as seed plants, bryophytes, ferns and fern allies.
Nonverbal	Nonverbal communications (NVC) is usually understood as the process of communication through sending and receiving wordless messages. NVC can be communicated through gesture and touch (Haptic communication), by body language or posture, by facial expression and eye contact. NVC can be communicated through object communication such as clothing, hairstyles or even architecture, symbols and infographics.

Nonverbal communication	Nonverbal communication is usually understood as the process of communication through sending and receiving wordless messages. i.e., language is not the only source of communication, there are other means also. NVC can be communicated through gestures and touch (Haptic communication), by body language or posture, by facial expression and eye contact.
Customer service	Customer service is the provision of service to customers before, during and after a purchase. According to Jamier L. Scott. (2002), `Customer service is a series of activities designed to enhance the level of customer satisfaction - that is, the feeling that a product or service has met the customer expectation.` Its importance varies by product, industry and customer; defective or broken merchandise can be exchanged, often only with a receipt and within a specified time frame.

Employment	Employment is a contract between two parties, one being the employer and the other being the employee. An employee may be defined as: `A person in the service of another under any contract of hire, express or implied, oral or written, where the employer has the power or right to control and direct the employee in the material details of how the work is to be performed.` Black`s Law Dictionary page 471 (5th ed. 1979). In a commercial setting, the employer conceives of a productive activity, generally with the intention of generating a profit, and the employee contributes labour to the enterprise, usually in return for payment of wages.
Equal	EQUAL was the `Community Initiative` within the European Social Fund of the European Union. It concerned `transnational co-operation to promote new means of combating all forms of discrimination and inEQUALities in connection with the labour market`. It ran from 2001 till 2007 with a budget of some â,¬3 billion of EU resources, matched by a similar sum from national resources.
Equal Employment Opportunity	The term Equal Employment Opportunity was created by President Lyndon B. Johnson when he signed Executive Order 11246 on September 24, 1965, created to prohibit federal contractors from discriminating against employees on the basis of race, sex, creed, religion, color, or national origin. In more recent times, most employers have also added sexual orientation to the list of non-discrimination. The Executive Order also required contractors to implement affirmative action plans to increase the participation of minorities and women in the workplace.
Equal Employment Opportunity Commission	The U.S. Equal Employment Opportunity Commission is an independent federal agency that enforces laws against workplace discrimination. The Equal Employment Opportunity Commission investigates discrimination complaints based on an individual`s race, color, national origin, religion, sex, sexual orentation, age, disability and retaliation for reporting and/or opposing a discriminatory practice. It is empowered to file discrimination suits against employers on behalf of alleged victims and to adjudicate claims of discrimination brought against federal agencies.
Performance appraisal	A Performance appraisal is a method by which the job performance of an employee is evaluated (generally in terms of quality, quantity, cost, and time) typically by the corresponding manager or supervisor. A Performance appraisal is a part of guiding and managing career development. It is the process of obtaining, analyzing, and recording information about the relative worth of an employee to the organization.

Behaviorally anchored rating scales	In psychology research on behaviorism, Behaviorally anchored rating scales are scales used to report performance. `Behaviorally anchored rating scales are normally presented vertically with scale points ranging from five to nine.`It is an appraisal method that aims to combine the benefits of narratives, critical incident incidents, and quantified ratings by anchoring a quantified scale with specific narrative examples of good or poor performance. BARS Behaviorally anchored rating scales is a method that combines elements of the traditional rating scales and critical incidents methods. In order to construct Behaviorally anchored rating scales seven steps are followed as mentioned below · Examples of effective and ineffective behavior related to job are collected from people with knowledge of job · These behaviors are converted in to performance dimensions · A group of participants will be asked to reclassify the incidents. At this stage the incidents for which there is not 75% agreement are discarded as being too subjective · Then the above mentioned incidents are rated from one to nine on a scale · Finally about six to seven incidents for each performance dimensions- all meeting retranslation and standard deviation criteria will be used as Behaviorally anchored rating scales. This is by far the best method used for a performance appraisal method
Nominative determinism	Nominative determinism refers to the theory that a person`s name is given an influential role in reflecting key attributes of his job, profession, but real examples are more highly prized, the more obscure the better.
Checklist	A Checklist is a type of informational job aid used to reduce failure by compensating for potential limits of human memory and attention. It helps to ensure consistency and completeness in carrying out a task. A basic example is the `to do list.` A more advanced Checklist would be a schedule, which lays out tasks to be done according to time of day or other factors.

360-degree feedback	In human resources or industrial/organizational psychology, 360-degree feedback is feedback that comes from all around an employee. `360` refers to the 360 degrees in a circle, with an individual figuratively in the center of the circle. Feedback is provided by subordinates, peers, and supervisors.
Management by objectives	Management by objectives is a process of agreeing upon objectives within an organization so that management and employees agree to the objectives and understand what they are in the organization. The term `Management by objectives` was first popularized by Peter Drucker in his 1954 book `The Practice of Management`. The essence of Management by objectives is participative goal setting, choosing course of actions and decision making. An important part of the Management by objectives is the measurement and the comparison of the employee`s actual performance with the standards set. Ideally, when employees themselves have been involved with the goal setting and choosing the course of action to be followed by them, they are more likely to fulfill their responsibilities.
Self-assessment	Self-assessment in an organisational setting, according to the EFQM definition, refers to a comprehensive, systematic and regular review of an organization`s activities and results referenced against the EFQM Excellence Model. The Self-assessment process allows the organization to discern clearly its strengths and areas in which improvements can be made and culminates in planned improvement actions which are then monitored for progress. Self-assessment in an educational setting involves students making judgments about their own work.
Financial statements	Financial statements (or financial reports) are formal records of the financial activities of a business, person, including United Kingdom company law, Financial statements are often referred to as accounts, although the term Financial statements is also used, particularly by accountants. Financial statements provide an overview of a business or person`s financial condition in both short and long term.

Brown	Brown is a color term, denoting a range of composite colors produced by a mixture of orange, red or yellow with black. The term is from Old English brún, in origin for any dusky or dark shade of color. The Common Germanic adjective *brûnoz, *brûnâ meant both dark colors and a glistening or shining quality, whence burnish.
Central tendency	In statistics, the term Central tendency relates to the way in which quantitative data tend to cluster around some value. A measure of Central tendency is any of a number of ways of specifying this \`central value\`. In practical statistical analyses, the terms are often used before one has chosen even a preliminary form of analysis: thus an initial objective might be to \`choose an appropriate measure of Central tendency\`.
Halo effect	The Halo effect is a cognitive bias whereby the perception of one trait is influenced by the perception of another trait (or several traits) of that person or object. An example would be judging a good-looking person as more intelligent. Halo effects happen especially if the perceiver does not have enough information about all traits, so that he makes assumptions based on one or two prominent traits--these one or two prominent traits \`overshadow\` other traits, similar to the radiation of light in optical Halo effects or halos in iconography (rings of light around someone\`s head).
Decision making	Decision making can be regarded as the mental processes resulting in the selection of a course of action among several alternatives. Every Decision making process produces a final choice. The output can be an action or an opinion of choice.
Employment discrimination	Employment discrimination is discrimination in hiring, promotion, job assignment, termination, and compensation. It includes various types of harassment. Many jurisdictions prohibit some types of Employment discrimination, often by forbidding discrimination based on certain traits (\`protected categories\`).
Brain drain	Brain drain or human capital flight is a large emigration of individuals with technical skills or knowledge, normally due to conflict, lack of opportunity, political instability, since emigrants usually take with them the fraction of value of their training sponsored by the government. It is a parallel of capital flight which refers to the same movement of financial capital.

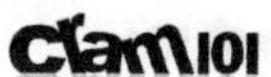

Regulations	The Control of Substances Hazardous to Health regulations 2002 is a United Kingdom Statutory Instrument that stipulates general requirements on employers to protect employees and other persons from the hazards of substances used at work by risk assessment, control of exposure, health surveillance and incident planning. There are also duties on employees to take care of their own exposure to hazardous substances and prohibitions on the import of certain substances into the European Economic Area. The regulations reenacted with amendements the Control of Substances Hazardous to Work regulations 1999 and implement several European Union directives.
Health Administration	Health administration is the field relating to leadership, management, and administration of hospitals, hospital networks, and health care systems. Health care administrators are considered health care professionals. The discipline is known by many names, including health management, healthcare management, health systems management, health care systems management, and medical and health services management.
Occupational Safety and Health Act	The Occupational Safety and Health Act is the primary federal law which governs occupational health and safety in the private sector and federal government in the United States. It was enacted by Congress in 1970 and was signed by President Richard Nixon on December 29, 1970. Its main goal is to ensure that employers provide employees with an environment free from recognized hazards, such as exposure to toxic chemicals, excessive noise levels, mechanical dangers, heat or cold stress, or unsanitary conditions. The Act can be found in the United States Code at title 29, chapter 15.
Chemical hazard	A Chemical hazard arises from contamination with harmful or potentially harmful chemicals. for example Burning of fossils, materials and chemicals used in construction and industry., the environment and water supply., chemical spillages and industrial accidents., deliberate releases.
Absenteeism	Absenteeism is a habitual pattern of absence from a duty or obligation. Frequent absence from the workplace may be indicative of poor morale or of sick building syndrome. However, many employers have implemented absence policies which make no distinction between absences for genuine illness and absence for inappropriate reasons.

Substance abuse	Substance abuse refers to a maladaptive pattern of use of a substance that is not considered dependent. The term `drug abuse` does not exclude dependency, but is otherwise used in a similar manner in nonmedical contexts. The terms have a huge range of definitions related to taking a psychoactive drug or performance enhancing drug for a non-therapeutic or non-medical effect.
Reduce	For example, it is fairly easy for a top executive to reduce the price of his/her company`s stock - due to information asymmetry. The executive can accelerate accounting of expected expenses, delay accounting of expected revenue, engage in off balance sheet transactions to make the company`s profitability appear temporarily poorer, or simply promote and report severely conservative (eg. pessimistic) estimates of future earnings.
Carpal tunnel syndrome	Carpal tunnel syndrome or median neuropathy at the wrist is a medical condition in which the median nerve is compressed at the wrist, leading to paresthesias, numbness and muscle weakness in the hand. Night symptoms and waking at night is a characteristic of established Carpal tunnel syndrome. They can be managed effectively with night-time wrist splinting in most patients.
Trade union	A Trade union is an organization of workers who have banded together to achieve common goals such as better working conditions. The Trade union, through its leadership, bargains with the employer on behalf of union members (rank and file members) and negotiates labour contracts (collective bargaining) with employers. This may include the negotiation of wages, work rules, complaint procedures, rules governing hiring, firing and promotion of workers, benefits, workplace safety and policies.
National Labor Relations Act	The National Labor Relations Act (or Wagner Act, after Robert F. Wagner) is a 1935 United States federal law that limits the means with which employers may react to workers in the private sector that labor unions, engage in collective bargaining, and take part in strikes and other forms of concerted activity in support of their demands. The Act does not, on the other hand, cover those workers who are covered by the Railway Labor Act, agricultural employees, domestic employees, supervisors, federal state or local government workers, independent contractors and some close relatives of individual employers. It was in a context of severe economic troubles that the Wagner Act came into effect.
Collective bargaining	Collective bargaining is a process between employers and employees to reach an agreement regarding the rights and duties of people at work. Collective bargaining aims to reach a collective agreement which usually sets out issues such as employees pay, working hours, training, health and safety, and rights to participate in workplace or company affairs.

	During the bargaining process, employees are typically represented by a trade union.
Union steward	Union Steward is the title of an official position within the organizational hierarchy of a labor union. Its uniqueness lies in the fact that rank-and-file members of the union hold this position voluntarily (through democratic election by fellow workers or sometimes by appointment of a higher union body) while maintaining their role as an employee of the firm. As a result, the Union Steward becomes a significant link and conduit of information between the union leadership and rank-and-file workers.
Age Discrimination in Employment Act	The Age Discrimination in Employment Act of 1967, Pub. L. No. 90-202, 81 Stat. 602 (Dec. 15, 1967), codified as Chapter 14 of Title 29 of the United States Code, 29 U.S.C. Â§ 621 through 29 U.S.C. Â§ 634 (ADEA), prohibits employment discrimination against persons 40 years of age or older in the United States). The law also sets standards for pensions and benefits provided by employers and requires that information about the needs of older workers be provided to the general public.
Age Discrimination in Employment Act of 1967	The Age Discrimination in Employment Act of 1967, Pub. L. No. 90-202, 81 Stat. 602 (Dec. 15, 1967), codified as Chapter 14 of Title 29 of the United States Code, 29 U.S.C. Â§ 621 through 29 U.S.C. Â§ 634 (ADEA), prohibits employment discrimination against persons 40 years of age or older in the United States). The law also sets standards for pensions and benefits provided by employers and requires that information about the needs of older workers be provided to the general public.
Sexual harassment	Sexual harassment is intimidation, bullying or coercion of a sexual nature, Sexual harassment may be illegal. It includes a range of behavior from seemingly mild transgressions and annoyances to actual sexual abuse or sexual assault.
Worker Adjustment and Retraining Notification Act	The Worker Adjustment and Retraining Notification Act is a United States labor law which protects employees, their families, and communities by requiring most employers with 100 or more employees to provide sixty- (60) calendar-day advance notification of plant closings and mass layoffs of employees. It was enacted in 1989. Employees entitled to notice under the Worker Adjustment and Retraining Notification Act include managers and supervisors, hourly wage, and salaried workers.
Plants	Plants are living organisms belonging to the kingdom Plantae. They include familiar organisms such as trees, herbs, bushes, grasses, vines, ferns, mosses, and green algae. The scientific study of plants, known as botany, has identified about 350,000 extant species of plants, defined as seed plants, bryophytes, ferns and fern allies.

Family and Medical Leave Act of 1993	The Family and Medical Leave Act of 1993 was signed into law on 5 February 1993 by President Bill Clinton . However, it did not take effect until August 5, 1993: a full six months after the president`s signature. The bill was among the first signed into law by President Clinton in his first term.
Uniformed Services Employment and Reemployment Rights Act	The Uniformed Services Employment and Reemployment Rights Act of 1994 (USERRA) was signed into law by U.S. President Bill Clinton on October 13, 1994 to protect the civilian employment of non-full time military service members in the United States called to active duty. The law applies to all United States uniformed services and their respective reserve components. USERRA clarifies and strengthens the Veterans` Reemployment Rights (VRR) Statute by protecting civilian job rights and benefits for veterans, members of reserve components, and even individuals activated by the President of the United States to provide Federal Response for National Emergencies.
Inventory	Inventory is a list for goods and materials, or those goods and materials themselves, held available in stock by a business. It is also used for a list of the contents of a household and for a list for testamentary purposes of the possessions of someone who has died. In accounting Inventory is considered an asset.
United States	The United States of America (commonly referred to as the United States, the U.S., the United StatesA, or America) is a federal constitutional republic comprising fifty states and a federal district. The country is situated mostly in central North America, where its forty-eight contiguous states and Washington, D.C., the capital district, lie between the Pacific and Atlantic Oceans, bordered by Canada to the north and Mexico to the south. The state of Alaska is in the northwest of the continent, with Canada to its east and Russia to the west across the Bering Strait.
Career	Career is a term defined by the Oxford English Dictionary as an individual`s `course or progress through life `. It is usually considered to pertain to remunerative work (and sometimes also formal education). The etymology of the term is somewhat ironic in that it comes from the Latin word carrera, which means race .
Workforce	The workforce is the labour pool in employment. It is generally used to describe those working for a single company or industry, but can also apply to a geographic region like a city, country, state, etc. The term generally excludes the employers or management, and implies those involved in manual labour.

Case study	A Case study is one of several ways of doing research whether it is social science related or even socially related. It is an intensive study of a single group, incident, or community. Other ways include experiments, surveys, or analysis of archival information.
Job hunting	Job hunting or job seeking is the act of looking for employment, due to unemployment or discontent with a current position. The immediate goal of job seeking is usually to obtain a job interview with an employer which may lead to getting hired. The job hunter or seeker typically first looks for job vacancies or employment opportunities. Common methods of Job hunting are: · using a job search engine · looking through the classifieds in newspapers · using a private or public employment agency or recruiter · finding a job through a friend or an extended business network or personal network · looking on a company`s web site for open jobs, typically in its applicant tracking system · going to a job fair It is expected the job seekers will have done a reasonable amount of research into the employers.
Resources	A resource is any physical or virtual entity of limited availability, or anything used to help one earn a living. In most cases, commercial or even ethic factors require resource allocation through resource management. As resources are very useful, we attach some information value to them.
Recruiter	A Recruiter is someone engaging in recruitment, or the solicitation of individuals to fill jobs or positions within a corporation, non-for-profit organization, sports team, etc. Recruiters may work within an organization`s Human Resources department (typically) or on an outsourced basis. Outsourced Recruiters typically work for multiple clients at once, on a third-party broker basis, and are variously called headhunters, search firms/agents, agency Recruiters, or recruitment consultants.

Informational Interview	An Informational interview is a meeting in which a job seeker asks for advice rather than employment. The job seeker uses the interview to gather information on the field, find employment leads and expand their professional network. This differs from a job interview because the job seeker asks the questions.
Hostile work environment	A Hostile work environment exists when an employee experiences workplace harassment and fears going to work because of the offensive, intimidating, religion, sex, national origin, age, disability, veteran status, or, in some jurisdictions, sexual orientation, political affiliation, citizenship status, marital status, or personal appearance. Hostile work environment is also one of the two legal categories of sexual harassment. A Hostile work environment may also be defined as when a boss or manager begins to engage in a manner designed to make you quit in retaliation for your actions.
Negotiations	The apartheid system in South Africa was ended through a series of negotiations between 1990 and 1993 and through unilateral steps by the De Klerk government. These negotiations took place between the governing National Party, the African National Congress, and a wide variety of other political organisations. negotiations took place against a backdrop of political violence in the country, including allegations of a state-sponsored third force destabilising the country.
Continuing education	Continuing education is an all encompassing term within a broad spectrum of post-secondary learning activities and programs. The term is used mainly in the United States. Recognized forms of post-secondary learning activities within the domain include: degree credit courses by non-traditional students, non-degree career training, workforce training, formal personal enrichment courses (both on-campus and online) self-directed learning (such as through Internet interest groups, clubs or personal research activities) and experiential learning as applied to problem solving.
Direct Marketing	Direct marketing is a sub-discipline and type of marketing. There are two main definitional characteristics which distinguish it from other types of marketing. The first is that it attempts to send its messages directly to consumers, without the use of intervening media.
Professional	A professional is a member of a vocation founded upon specialised educational training. The word professional traditionally means a person who has obtained a degree in a professional field. The term professional is used more generally to denote a white collar working person, or a person who performs commercially in a field typically reserved for hobbyists or amateurs.

Social responsibility	Social responsibility is an ethical or ideological theory that an entity whether it is a government, corporation, organization or individual has a big responsibility to society at large. This responsibility can be `negative`, meaning there is exemption from blame or liability, or it can be `positive,` meaning there is a responsibility to act beneficently (proactive stance). Businesses can use ethical decision making to secure their businesses by making decisions that allow for government agencies to minimize their involvement with the corporation.

CPSIA information can be obtained at www.ICGtesting.com
Printed in the USA
LVOW010508150812

294391LV00001B/72/P

9 781428 878150